FREELANCE WRITING EXPRESS

How to Earn
$$$
Within Two Weeks

Darlene Elizabeth Williams

ISBN-10: 1512283053
ISBN-13: 978-1512283051

DEDICATION

This book is dedicated to the three greatest loves of my life: My husband, Joe, and my sons, Bryan and Matthew. God has blessed me indeed.

TABLE OF CONTENTS

ACKNOWLEDGEMENTS

My gratitude to my husband, Joe, Alison McQuillan, Writers of Non-Fiction (Facebook group), and my treasured fiction colleagues for their unwavering support and belief in me. Thank you for not letting me give up.

This book would be incomplete without mentioning and giving thanks to the following, who provided valuable input, advice, and assistance:

Book Mentor: Denise Michaels
Cover designer: Ares Yun
Proofreader: Joseph Guetre
Formatter: Rich Meyer
Photographer: Sue Freeman, Portrait Art Photography

FOREWORD

This book changed my life!

How often have you read a claim you can earn money immediately freelance writing and rolled your eyes?

You are right to be skeptical except, in this case, this statement happens to be true.

After seventeen years in the same job and altered family circumstances, I needed a change. I was uncertain which direction to take. I met Darlene several years ago on Facebook. When Darlene posted she was seeking beta mentoring students for her program based on *Freelance Writing Express ~ How to Earn $$$ Within Two Weeks*, I jumped at the opportunity.

The rest, as the cliché goes, is history.

I followed Darlene's sage advice and targeted my writing at a few niche areas of personal interest, and it worked. Two months ago, I gave up the day job, and last month my income was comfortably into four figures—and is still climbing. I write about what I love—animals—and get paid for it.

Without Darlene's knowledge of the freelance market, I would never have known where to start or had the courage to take the leap. *Freelance Writing Express* taught me to ignore the blind alleyways and start working like a pro.

I am proof that, with a great profile and a little preparatory work, you too can earn a good income freelance writing. Let's face it: if a cautious person like myself can do it—anyone can.

Pippa Elliott
October 2014

INTRODUCTION

"First say to yourself what you would be; and then do what you have to do."

~ Epictetus, Discourses, c. AD 100

An author recently read the title of this book. She laughed, pointed at "How to Earn $$$ Within Two Weeks", and said, "I don't believe that."

At first I was indignant, then I realized that if she read this book, she would recognize the validity of this statement.

Freelance Writing Express is different than all the other how-to books about freelance writing. I take you step-by-step through the process of establishing your career through concise, yet comprehensive, instructions. You will have earnings in your bank account within two weeks. Read on and you will soon discover why Freelance Writing Express is the perfect answer as a strategic approach to a career as a freelance writer, and the answer to the multitude of questions that accompany a new occupation. I presume you purchased this book because you are either an aspiring freelance writer or, perhaps, have already commenced your career but discovered it difficult to land writing gigs. You are not alone. There are scads of freelance writers who are in the same position as you. As once was I. As a newbie to the freelance writing world, I was ignorant of scams, petty-pay web content mills, and felt desperate within a short time that I would ever make any money—let alone a living—in a bewildering world. Months were wasted conducting research about how to become a successful freelance writer. There is no shortage of blogs dishing advice. I read everything, Googled a hundred different word variations, and still came up empty and right back where I began. What I never did find was informative, actionable advice from writers in the trench that anyone and everyone could apply.

This is why I chose to write *Freelance Writing Express*. I developed a system that worked for me, and can work equally successfully for you. What differentiates *Freelance Writing Express*? I honestly believe anyone can utilize my experience and methods to start their freelance writing career without the steep learning curve. I have eliminated the blog posts, Google searches, scams, and pennies-per-hour content mills. Through *Freelance Writing Express*, I lay out in concise detail how to write your first articles for money within the next week, two weeks, or however long it takes you to work your way through the steps.

There is nothing in *Freelance Writing Express* that is impossible for you to accomplish. I do not have a university degree. I did not take writing courses. What I do have are life experiences and an insatiable curiosity. There are copywriting online courses that make promises which never come true. I investigated them thoroughly. They take your money and promise you gigs at the end of the course. The problem being, of course, there are no writing gigs. Experienced clientele and other writers know that course you invested in is shoddy and not worth the lovely certificate you print when you complete the program.

It is not my goal with *Freelance Writing Express* to hand out advice I would not take myself. This is the nuts and bolts of how to kick start your career. There are no

"Earn a Living as a Freelance Writer! No special skills needed! Easy and Fun! Start today and get paid tomorrow! Work your own hours! Write wherever you want to! Look at me writing at the poolside in Mexico and earning a 6 figure income! Take vacations any time you want!" messages in this book. These enticements bombarding hapless freelance writers are plain and simple—for lack of a more apt descriptive term—garbage.

Stay with *Freelance Writing Express*. I guarantee I will not direct you to write one word for free. Each step in the process is geared towards ensuring you earn money for every piece you write. Sometimes, I dispense hard facts that might feel uncomfortable, but I do this for your benefit. Stretching your comfort zone is the only way to grow as a writer. Challenges soon become second nature and your writing skills improve immensely. *Freelance Writing Express* is your solution to establishing your career, setting tangible goals, setting realistic expectations, earning money for every word you write, growth as a writer, and support every step of the journey.

CHAPTER 1
THE FACTS ABOUT THE FREELANCE WRITING WORLD

"People who like this sort of thing will find this the sort of thing they like."
~ Abraham Lincoln, quoted in G.W.E. Russell, Collections and Recollections, 1898

This chapter deals with myths and facts. You will learn what the true writing world environment is all about, whether your vision as a freelance writer is on target, and what you can expect from me, as your mentor, as we progress through *Freelance Writing Express*. Succinct writing is optimal. *Freelance Writing Express* is written with this in mind. There is no filler or fluff; only direct, honest facts. I have read many how-to books that left me with the feeling I learned nothing, but, somehow, the author managed to fill 200 pages. Be it an article, blog post, or book, always keep in mind fluff and filler fools no one.

The first myth we deal with is a typical claim: "No Skills Required!" Without skills, I promise you will make zero money. Writing is an occupation. Just as with any employment vocation, you absolutely require skillsets. Imagine you decide to teach elementary school, but hold no university degree. The odds of obtaining a teacher's position are slim to none. The same is true with writing.

Sure anybody can string a sentence together. The question is: How does that sentence read? Does it make sense? Is it grammatically correct? Are there spelling errors? Is it relevant? Is it informative and factual? All of the above questions separate the wheat from the chaff. If a writer cannot fulfill every single point and is not interested in learning how to, he or she should look for a different career. *Freelance Writing Express* is not going to teach you how to write. This book is for writers who have mastered basic writing skills and are ambitious to establish their career and grow. Another misconception touted by content mills is "writing is easy".

Lousy writing is easy; professional writing is not. In the beginning, you likely will write slowly until you gain confidence and your writing chops mature. As time goes on, the writing comes faster and easier. This does not mean there is ever a point where you stop striving to improve your writing. If your writing stagnates, your career follows in a downward spiral. "Choose your own hours!" is another popular tagline. This ambiguous statement indicates you do not have to work 9-5 and go home at the end of the shift, only to wake up the next morning to the same routine. Certainly you can choose your own hours, but you still need to work a certain amount of hours at some point. If you are at your best in the early morning, get up at 4 AM and hit the keyboard. Similarly for night owls, 10 PM works too. Or mid-morning or afternoon. The choice is yours. The only caveat is you need to calculate how many hours you must work per day or week to obtain your financial objective. Unless you are currently unemployed or retired, it is best not to give your employer notice until you have established your name as a freelance writer. Writing is not an instant flow of work and income. That comes later when you have earned yourself a reputation as an excellent writer and clients are knocking on your figurative door. How much later? It all depends on you and the effort you invest. While we are talking about reputations, I should mention freelance writing will not make you a household name. Rarely, if ever, are you offered a byline for your work. You might not become famous, but you can be well-known within the freelance writing community as an excellent writer, who thoroughly researches topics, writes informative and compelling content, delivers on time, and requires no edits. Clients love this!

Momentum is the key word to remember. One step leads to another and another. In time, all those little steps garner you referrals, recommendations, and repeat clients. How long this takes is individualistic. There are no set guidelines due to variables, which include clientele retention, your subject matter expertise, supply and demand, and—not ever to be forgotten—the intense competition. Can you earn a six figure income freelance writing? Some writers do, some do not. Will you earn a comfortable living or extra pocket money? I truly believe it is possible to bring in a decent income if you dedicate yourself and pursue opportunities relentlessly. I am not going to throw numbers around as, in the end, they are meaningless. What constitutes an affluent lifestyle to one individual may not be the vision of another. Such a concept is undefinable.

A quote I find especially encouraging is:

> *"You don't always have to be the best, the most high profile or the most well-connected freelancer to be a success: average can be more than enough. It can even be exceptional."*

I spent countless hours when I launched my own career researching how to market myself. I encountered all of the aforementioned glamorous taglines. I fell for some and learned the unpalatable truth with my first project. I rewrote 40 articles for $40. I figured if I could just get started with one project, I could go onto bigger and better assignments. By the time I finished rewriting horribly written articles, I had spent hours earning about $1 an hour. It did not lead to better paying projects. In fact, the client was quite impressed with my work and he offered me more—at the same pay rate. It was a hard lesson, but I learned from it.

The truth is freelance writing has a steep learning curve. The enticing landing pages that offer you, the writer, the opportunity to earn limitless income, work your own hours, churn out web content with no skills required, and have a party doing it, are attempts to hoodwink you into membership cash grabs. These content mills ensnare writers, who are then apprehensive of leaving for greener pastures for fear of not earning any income. The vast majority of these mills have few projects up for grabs.

Freelance Writing Express focusses on freelance writing sources where you really can earn income. Dependent upon development of your knowledge base, research skills, writing abilities, communications savvy, and organization and discipline capabilities (all of which are discussed in-depth in this book), an hourly estimate of between $20 to $30 or higher is not unreasonable. One of the income sources I cover frequently offers $45 to $50 for a 500 word article. That is an hour of your time.

I promised to tell you what you can expect from me, as your mentor. I will be with you from the first step to lead you through setting up shop, developing your expertise, researching, writing and selling your first article, and beyond.

Quick Summary

- Succinct writing is optimal
- You must be willing to grow as a writer
- Professional writing requires dedication
- You must write a calculated amount of hours daily or weekly
- Your reputation is dependent on the quality of your work
- You will meet your income goals
- Freelance writing has a steep learning curve
- Content mills trap writers
- *Freelance Writing Express* guides you to a successful career
- I am with you every step

Up next, the pros and cons of freelance writing! Hint: there are more positives than negatives.

CHAPTER 2
Pros and Cons of Freelance Writing

"Exit, pursued by bear"
~ William Shakespeare, The Winter's Tale

In this chapter, we explore the pros and cons of freelance writing. At the end of this chapter, take time to consider the information. Most will decide freelance writing is definitely their career choice, but a few might have reservations.

That is okay. It is a huge step in your life, especially if you decide to make freelance writing your full-time career, and this is worthy of reflection on whether this is your right pathway. Let us get the ugly out of the way first. In this section, I list drawbacks to professional freelance writing: You are responsible for the operation of all elements of a business. There are inevitable administrative tasks that must be attended to, whether they are enjoyable or not. At all times, you must keep in mind this is a business and treat it as such. There are many hats to wear: bookkeeper, paying accounts, marketing, purchasing supplies, preparing appropriate tax forms, submitting income tax. Many of us are gifted in the creative aspect, but find daily administrative tasks tedious. If you are a social animal, the isolation that goes hand in glove with freelance writing might be difficult. This is a tough one: no guaranteed paycheck. You must be extremely proactive in searching for projects and marketing yourself. If you are having a difficult time with an assignment, you are on your own to figure out how to tackle it or find solutions. If any element of professional writing—researching, writing, editing, proofreading—does not appeal to you, or you have weaknesses in these areas, freelance writing might not be the best choice.

Client relations are paramount. Most clients are great, some are not. If the prospect of dealing with unreasonable clients dismays you, or your personality does not lend itself to customer relations, you might find freelance writing a challenge. This occupation comes without health benefits, although you might want to check out the Freelancers Union to see what benefits are available and the costs. The union offers health, dental, disability, life insurance, and retirement options. Availability is based on your zip code. Accordingly, benefits may vary. Family and friends, for some reason, often do not take your occupation seriously. You are typically home all day and interruptions by others are a given unless you put your foot down firmly and lay down rules. Organizational and discipline skills are a must. These principles must be adhered to steadfastly. The good news about the above drawbacks is, if you are aware of what is involved, you can educate or prepare yourself for these eventualities. None are insurmountable if you are determined freelance writing is your ultimate career.

Now for the terrific stuff: You write and are paid for it! You enjoy full authority over your career. You invest as much time as you want or have available, and take it in whichever direction you choose. While you may have to establish a baseline financial goal, the world is your oyster. However you arrive at a monetary figure is completely your choice. Please do keep in mind, however, the caveats mentioned in the Introduction and Chapter 1. Keep your goals realistic. No commute. No career clothes. No gas expenditures. Three big bonuses rolled into one. Tired of office politics? You decide when to raise your rates, not when your boss finally figures they can no longer put off a raise and still keep you around. Flexibility. You choose what hours you write. They can vary daily to take into account your family and/or social life and what time of the day (or night) you are at your optimum. Freedom to choose projects consistent with your interests and expertise. Do be aware you might have to take on a few projects where your heart and soul do not lay to achieve your financial goals.

Learn about fascinating subjects. Every writer should love to learn. It is what freelance writing is all about: educating yourself and then others through your writing. An extra bonus is you become a veritable cornucopia of trivia, which makes for excellent conversation starters. Fulfillment through your success. No waiting for the boss to pat you on the shoulder and say "well done". You alone earned the kudos. It is a phenomenal feeling to finish a project knowing you have exceeded your client's (and sometimes your own) expectations. We have done a run through of the most common drawbacks and bonuses of freelance writing. Now is the time to reflect:

Do you want to be responsible for every detail operating your own business? Do the benefits outweigh the disadvantages? Do you want to be a freelance writer so fervently you are willing to overcome all obstacles?

Quick Summary
- There are pros and cons to freelance writing
- You must weigh the factors to make a decision
- You can overcome obstacles

Only you can fathom the answers to these questions.

If you are passionate about writing, I already know your response. That is why the next chapter is all about setting up your business.

CHAPTER 3
Setting up Shop

"A good beginning makes a good ending."
~ Anonymous (English Proverb)

This chapter demonstrates how easy and inexpensive it is to set up a freelance writing business. Aside from a few major feature requirements, working from home entails low overhead costs, with the beauty of income tax write-offs.

Computer

The most important items required are a reliable computer and internet services. I personally prefer to use a laptop computer because of its portability. Working as a freelance writer can be a mobile career if you choose.

Numerous times I take my laptop with me on out-of-town trips and complete work if deadlines are looming. If you already own a computer, it does not need to have all the latest features, which can be pricey. I worked on an older version for years.

If you need to purchase a computer for your freelance writing career, explain to the salesperson exactly what you are using the computer for. The computer you need to support a good word processing software will be in the mid-price point category. I do recommend a screen wide enough to support viewing two pages simultaneously, so you can view your work page and research page side-by-side. Alternatively, some writers prefer to have two monitors.

Internet

A dependable Internet services provider is invaluable. Do your research before signing up. The cheapest provider can cost you anxiety in meeting work deadlines and money from prospective projects if service is frequently down. Quite simply put, you may have to pay more for an Internet provider to ensure constant and consistent internet access.

A freelance writer cannot work without the internet. When I opened Clayton Freelance Writing Services, I had difficulties with Internet access which resulted in numerous lengthy calls to support services. This put me behind schedule on my projects. I often ended up working late at night to catch up to meet deadlines. This is an added stress you do not need. I switched providers immediately.

Word Processing Software

For PC owners, Microsoft Home Office Edition is more than adequate and, for Mac owners, Microsoft for Mac is likely your best bet. You must be able to share your documents and the two formats noted are the most popular.

Word processing software can be purchased and downloaded from the Internet or purchased from a retailer. Downloading is convenient, but having the backup disk can prove invaluable if your computer crashes. If you decide to download, ascertain whether a backup disk is available. This is often possible for a nominal fee.

File Backup

Speaking of computer crashes, backup of files is

essential. Imagine you have written fifty articles due in two days and are polishing them. Your computer crashes. Disaster. It will be impossible to rewrite these articles by the deadline.

There are several free options to ensure you are never in this situation. OneDrive, iCloud, Dropbox, and Google Drive are dependable and safe to upload your documents. You can also access your documents from any computer or device anytime and anywhere.

Copyscape

Copyscape is an online software tool that detects plagiarism. Plagiarism is frequently an unconscious occurrence. Every piece of content you write needs to be checked for plagiarism. More to come about Copyscape in Chapter 10.

Office Furniture

Ideally, a desk is optimum. However, a reasonably sized table will suffice. Sufficient work space for your computer, printer, supplies, files, and a work area where a file can be fully opened are all considerations. You may feel overwhelmed trying to work in a jumble of papers with supplies scattered over your work surface. If you are strapped for cash, cruise used furniture stores where desks are commonly sold cheap.

You will spend many hours sitting on a computer chair. An unsuitable chair causes fatigue, muscle pain, and can lead to more serious problems, such as carpel tunnel syndrome. Make sure your chair supports your lumbar spine, is height adjustable, your feet are flat on the ground, and you are comfortable overall. This does not necessarily have to be expensive. Some of the lower-priced chairs will suit you perfectly. Sit in every one in the store before you make up your mind.

If possible, purchase a filing cabinet or, at the very least, file sorters. The drawback to file sorters is the large amount of space they occupy. I use a filing cabinet where I store completed file projects and a file sorter for ongoing projects. Filing cabinets can be picked up for less than $5 at garage sales.

General Office Supplies

General supplies basic to any office environment include:

- Stapler
- Calculator
- Black, blue, and red pens
- Pencils
- Stick it notes
- Multiple colored sets of file folders (one color for each writing source and one for administrative)
- Prong fasteners (for files)
- 2 Hole Punch
- Ledger book or bookkeeping software
- Printer ink
- Paper

Buying in bulk, especially paper and printer ink, saves you money long term, even if it seems a considerable outlay in the beginning. I purchase office supplies from warehouse retailers. It is eventually used; it is not money squandered, it is money conserved.

Use both sides of paper for twice the mileage. Projects are delivered virtually. No one but you is ever going to see the actual printed version. Every penny hoarded from earnings goes into your pocket. I run a cost-efficient business.

PayPal

Speaking of earnings, you need to open a PayPal account. Project fees are transferred from income sources into your PayPal account. If you happen to land a gig independent of these sites, you should always invoice the client through PayPal. Do not fall for the "Western Union money order scam".

PayPal is free to use, although if you withdraw amounts less than $150.00 there is a small charge. All your earnings will be in United States currency and PayPal converts into your country's currency, if you are not a US resident.

If you have independent clients, PayPal charges an invoice service fee. Calculate the amount (it is based on a percentage of the total invoice amount) and add it to the invoice. I have never had a client squabble about the additional charge.

As you can see, the financial outlay is indeed minimal. You probably have most of the necessities already. If it takes a few paid projects before you obtain everything you need, so be it.

Quick Summary
- A reliable computer is vital
- Dependable Internet is crucial
- Word processing software is a necessity
- File backup is essential (free)
- Plagiarism software is required (free)
- Comfortable, spacious office furniture is important
- You need only minimal office supplies (buy in bulk if possible)
- Open a PayPal account

The next chapter concentrates on the "boss" word.

CHAPTER 4
CEO, BOSS, COMMANDER, CHIEF, TYCOON—YOU CHOOSE

"Procrastination is the thief of time."
~ Edward Young, Night Thoughts, 1742-45

Ah, the beauty of being your own boss. No one to tell you what and when to do something, especially a task you do not enjoy. All those poor employees shackled to specified work hours, limited vacation days, and a boss who is an idiot. You have the best of worlds; in a word: freedom. Now, let me bring you back from fantasy land to reality. You have to locate clients, negotiate projects, placate the unreasonable client, fulfill deadlines, order supplies, maintain accounts, and a myriad of other small details you probably never noticed as an employee. Plus, there is no underling to shift blame onto if something goes sideways. I have worked both sides of the fence. I will take self-employed any day of the week. Self-employment takes discipline, which can be a somewhat tough attribute to assimilate, ambition, and the chutzpah to carry on when the going gets rough. The love of what I do has driven me to adopt all of this and more. Now down to the nitty-gritty (with a bonus at the end):

Discipline

Discipline is a double-edged sword. It can be either the noun: "a trained condition of order"; or, the verb: "punishment". This might make you think of a parental situation where children are trained to obey or children are punished for disobedience. In the freelance writing world, practicing discipline earns you money. A lack of discipline earns you the "punishment" of a dearth of clients. Either way, there are consequences. You must make a conscious decision about which meaning you apply to your career. Let us examine common principles of discipline of self-employment or running a business:

Sit in your chair in front of the computer.

This may sound like a stupid piece of advice but, until you have to do it every day whether you feel like it or not, it can be one of the hardest principles to follow. If you have worked a "traditional" job as an employee, you know if you do not show up, you are out of a job. The same applies to freelance writing, but it might take you a little longer than a couple of days to realize you have lost your job. There is no boss to hover over you to ensure you work your designated hours and the freedom "to choose your hours" can be tempting.

Prioritize.

Attacking your projects willy-nilly is the worst possible tactic. Before long you are no longer in control of anything. Deadlines are your number one priority. Fill in smaller tasks around set-in-stone dates, or break down a large project into less intimidating chunks. If it seems I harp about deadlines, you are correct. I do. One missed deadline and a complaint from a client can forever haunt you.

Utilize a scheduling system.

The type of scheduling system you use does not matter as long as it works for you. From my days as a legal assistant and pre-technological advances, I used a daily agenda book and two colored pens. The non-technologically challenged might cringe at my old school agenda book, but it has worked for me for over twenty years. Unless it actually burned, there is no way I will lose reminders and deadlines. In law, a missed date is enough to have a case thrown out of court and the law firm assessed costs. Most definitely not something I wanted to be responsible for, especially if I hoped to continue in that field. There are many options available. Investigate and choose one that suits you best, use it, and make sure it is backed up every night.

Preplan your work.

At the end of the day, write down your writing goals for the next day in order of priority in your scheduling system. The next day, immediately work on the list without deviation. You wrote the list in a particular order the previous day for a reason. No switching up items on the list is permitted. Repeat ad nauseam until it becomes second nature.

Get the "I don't want to this" stuff done first.

Perform your ugliest task first thing in the morning. The one obligation you wish you never had to look at again. For me, it is bookkeeping. Accounting for a freelance writing professional is filled with petty little entries. The mere thought of entering sometimes mere pennies into the ledger is an anathema. Numbers and I do not get along. We have now called an armed truce. I keep my accounting current. The pain of backtracking expenses and income for several weeks (okay, months) is not worth avoidance of ten minutes maximum each day.

Terminate Procrastination

Procrastination is an avoidance behavior. Almost everyone procrastinates about something in their life. It is typically a task you fear or do not relish. It could be sorting papers that need to be filed, laundry, paying bills. The list is endless.

The official definition of procrastination is "the act or habit of putting things off till later; delay." Procrastination in freelance writing has unpleasant ramifications.

The freelance writer often juggles projects with staggered deadlines. It is easy to choose a project you feel comfortable writing. You might have a fair amount of knowledge already about the subject at hand, or know research is plentiful.

If you work on those projects you feel confident with, the project you avoid because you are anxious about the subject matter and its difficulty weighs on your mind. While you work on other projects, that challenging project you put off plays constant havoc with your subconscious. This is counter-productive. One of the most challenging projects I received regarded linguistics. I knew nothing about linguistics and, when I delved into the subject, I quickly discovered the complexity of linguistics. It is akin to reading a foreign language in English. The dictionary sat next to me while I tried to make sense of what I was reading. That project took a long time to write; far longer than I anticipated. Procrastination had reared its ugly head. I was falling behind on other work with short deadlines in order to make the deadline on the linguistics.

The effect of procrastination snowballs. You fall behind on one project and, all of a sudden, you are scrambling to meet deadlines on your other projects. You become overwhelmed.

A swamped writer, or anyone in any occupation for that

matter, does not perform well. You are unable to focus properly on the work at hand. You fret about several projects rather than just one.

I am going to share another experience. When I wrote this section, my file overflowed with research and ideas. I sat with a mountain of topics and valuable information to include in this book.

The realization of the monumental project I intended to undertake prostrated me. I sat frozen in front of a computer with a blank screen. I sorted materials in my file instead. Procrastination.

I decided this was the perfect topic to write about first. Then I made a pact with myself I would write a minimum 500 words per day before I gave into the temptation to work on my social media platform or do the laundry.

It is vital to recognize procrastination behavior. Then it is crucial you counteract those impulses. Write that project that scares you first. Get the most onerous task out of the way. You feel incredible relief it is finished, along with elation you conquered a formidable obstacle. Now you can continue with those other projects untroubled by nagging background distractions.

Right now I have a euphoric sense of achievement. The first 575 words of this project written in less than 45 minutes. My colossal undertaking has launched. Now I can move forward.

Always check in with yourself to ensure you are not engaging in detrimental procrastination behavior. If you need encouragement, reread the next section *Go Get 'em-Setting Goals* until you have the proper mindset.

Go Get 'em—Setting Goals

Too many people commence their businesses without clear objectives in mind. Setting goals and striving to attain those targets with a tangible plan is paramount.

You need to incorporate the ethics and values talked about below into your business plan to reach your ultimate destination—success: *First and foremost is take responsibility for your actions*. You are your business. A happy client is a result of your actions. A not-so-pleased client is similarly a culmination of your endeavors. Give that client excellently written content, and you have a satisfied customer who may come back for more. Miss a deadline, and you have a disgruntled client who writes a poor performance review. *Recognize grunt work is a necessity*. Attack it with enthusiasm. This is not particularly appealing, but putting in the extra effort pays off. Do not have the attitude loathsome details are beneath you. It is those small details that make you stand out from the crowd. *Stretch that comfort zone*. Your business growth stagnates if you are unwilling to take on a particular project, learn a new system or software, or educate yourself on a new topic. Yes, it is uncomfortable. You might fear failure. What is guaranteed if you do not give it a shot? Failure. Thriving businesses are the result of failures and lessons learned. Believe in yourself without reservation. You can stretch your comfort zone and experience setbacks, but be confident you can master what you set out to achieve.

Modest steps transform into abundant opportunities.

Sensibility dictates there is no such thing as a "quantum leap". Behind every so-called quantum leap are repeated small adjustments and improvements that eventually magnify to where it appears a person happened to be in the right place at the right time, an opportunity dropped into their lap, or just plain good luck. You might be the only person who notices these miniscule advances for a period of time. That is okay. There comes a time in the near future where, if you continually work on these slight refinements, people sit up and take notice of your exemplary skills. *Tenacity wins the day*. Doggedly—but politely and tactfully—pursue projects or clients you know you can offer superior service. It may take several attempts but, the more frequently a client sees your name, he or she knows you are bent on proving you are the perfect writer for their projects. Persistence might well win you a long-term relationship. *Under-promise and over-deliver*. Nothing delights a client more than receiving a project earlier than the due date. Turning in a project past the due date guarantees you most probably lost a client.

Self-reliance proves your value.

As far as possible, without compromising the project, take the reins and run with the project. Constant messages to the client over details which a savvy writer should be able to figure out are an annoyance. Keep in mind, although, not all clients understand the type of instructions required. If the project description is too vague, a message to the client is certainly in order. Another method of confirming you and the client are on the same page is to write the first article and send it to the client requesting confirmation you are headed in the right direction. *Focus*. Give your full attention to the project or task at hand. Haphazard attention produces substandard results.

Professionalism at all times indicates to the client a proficient expert is at work on their project.

The client is then assured their project is in good hands. Prove to the client their confidence is not misplaced.

Track your progress and monitor feedback.

It is essential to track your progress. If a certain task is taking up too much of your time, explore why. Research that aspect to gain a better understanding of how to tackle it in a timely manner. Similarly, if you receive several complaints of the same nature from various clients, it is imperative you sit down and draw up a plan to negate these types of comments in the future.

Never stop learning.

There is always something new to consider or learn. No one person knows it all. Take the combined knowledge of several sources and apply it to your freelance writing career. You have gained valuable knowledge even if you only take away one new concept per week from a freelance writing blog.

Adaptability is essential.

Nothing stands still in today's world. You need to stay on top of changes and understand them. Some are irrelevant, others may be important. You need to give all changes your attention to decide which are applicable to you and your career. Despite all of the advice above, you must maintain a healthy work/life balance. Working yourself to the bone does no one favors, especially you. If you have to say "no" to a project because it is impossible to fit into your schedule, so be it. You might lose that client or he/she may be willing to wait for your schedule to free up. There are always clients who think they are your only client and expect you to drop everything immediately to work on their project. Pandering to these clients reinforces their position.

I had a client who expected me to put him ahead of everyone else. When I reached the point where I was saturated and barely keeping my head above water, I told him it was a three week wait. I never heard from him again.

Was it really a loss? No. I had enough work that I, quite frankly, was glad to be rid of him. He was a demanding client with unreasonable expectations. He was a professional himself, but unable to accept he was not my only client.

Had I attempted to accommodate him, I would have had zero balance in my life. If you are not living a healthy lifestyle, it is guaranteed you will burn out. Family time, social events, eating healthy, and physical exercise all keep you in top physical and emotional shape to run a profitable business.

The content market demand is monumental, and it is only going to increase in the years to come. Technology and economics are and will remain driving factors.

Finally, do not forget to give the boss a nice reward every once in a while for a great job done!

Quick Summary

Freelance writing requires discipline, prioritization, a scheduling system, and preplanning. Procrastination is disastrous Setting goals takes responsibility and includes grunt work, stretching your comfort zone, modest steps forward, tenacity, self-reliance, focus, professionalism, and adaptability. A healthy work/life balance is necessary to prevent burnout The content market is in huge demand and growing Now we have the business aspects of freelance writing out of the way, we can now move on to the actual mechanics of writing.

Next chapter we start with examining the traits of an excellent writer, with a little grammar thrown in.

CHAPTER 5
TRAITS OF AN EXCELLENT WRITER—WITH A LITTLE GRAMMAR THROWN IN

"There is no way of writing well and also of writing easily."
~ Anthony Trollope, Barchester Towers, 1857

Writing is hard work. Excellent writing skills are not something that come naturally. We all have to strive to improve our writing. How do you do that? By writing. The more you write, the better you become. You probably have natural talent—that is why you want to become a freelance writer—but that innate ability requires constant development.

Traits of an Excellent Writer
An excellent writer needs three capabilities:
- Cognitive skills
- Mechanical skills
- Stylistic Skills

Cognitive skills:
Involve the ability to draw pertinent facts from research and summarize them in a cohesive manner, with supportive evidence to verify what you state to be the truth.

For instance, if you are writing an article about the Great Wall of China, you need to separate myths from facts. There are several sites on the Internet that claim bodies of workers are buried beneath the wall as "filler". Dig a little deeper, and you discover this to be a myth. There is no scientific evidence there are any skeletons within the Great Wall.

If a writer went with the first source claiming bodies were used as foundation building "material", the article contains inaccuracies. Send such an article to your client and watch how fast the client drops you.

Mechanical skills:

Are varying the length and structure of sentences, paragraphs, and maintaining a continuous thread throughout the articles. Your article should logically follow a thought process that provides the reader with a cohesive picture of the information. For instance, an article describing a medical procedure should begin with what to expect, how the operation is conducted, recovery care, and any post-operative alerts to prompt you to follow up with your surgeon.

Stylistic skills:

Are all about presentation. The tone of the article, wording, grammatical accuracy, and correct word choices all fall within stylistic guidelines. The writer must ensure there are no ambiguities that might unintentionally mislead the reader.

This may seem daunting if you are a novice freelance writer, but these skills do develop with time and effort. The level of effort decreases as you become more comfortable with your skills set.

Grammar

Which brings us to the topic of grammar. The subject most of us love to hate. Unfortunately, it is a vital topic freelance writers ignore at their peril.

I am not suggesting you become a grammar guru capable of identifying every grammatical term and dissecting sentences. What I am proposing is solid basic grammar skills.

We have all seen poorly written website content. What kind of impression does that leave? Are you interested in reading the entire article? Do you think the organization or individual is the professional they claim to be? Not likely.

When you write an article for a client, you must portray yourself as an expert in that field. What is the best method of conveying you expertise? Quality writing.

Basic skills required are excellent spelling, punctuation, and grammar. Spell check and grammar check are great starter tools, but they are not infallible. Invaluable resources to have in your arsenal are:

- The Elements of Style by William Strunk and E.B. White (a must-have classic)
- Merriam-Webster's Collegiate Dictionary, Eleventh Edition (Merriam-Webster continually updates and revises the Eleventh Edition. Be sure you have the most recent edition. At the time of writing—2014—a revised edition has just been released. My copy is from 2012. I read 150 new words were added. I will not purchase a new edition based on 150 new words, but I will keep my eye open for further revisions so that, when a substantial amount of new words are added, I will then purchase it.)
- The Chicago Manual of Style, 16th Edition
- Associated Press Stylebook 2014

- American Psychology Association Guidelines
- Random House Word Menu
- Garner's Modern American Usage

These resource materials should become well-thumbed as you progress with your writing career.

Two plagues still challenge me when writing: word repetition and extraneous wording. It is something every writer does. What you need to do is recognize your own personal blights.

The word "that" is my personal repetitious word bane. After I write an article, I go back and remove every unnecessary "that".

A simple method of finding repetitious words or phrases is pressing Ctrl+F simultaneously. Type in the word or phrase. This command searches your entire document and lists every instance where the offending word or phrase is located.

You can then edit each sentence in which it appears to eliminate it, if practicable.

Extraneous wording is what I call "fluff" and "filler". Some writers pad their articles with modifiers to make the word count. I am adamantly against this practice.

Unnecessary modifiers are a typical example. Words, such as:

Almost	Often
Always	Only
Big	Pretty
Hardly	Quite
Just	Too
Little	So
Many	Such
More	Very

Much

...are all unnecessary and extraneous modifiers. Sometimes, a modifier is necessary to present correct information. Ensure you do not alter the meaning of a sentence by stripping all modifiers automatically.

The following text—and corrections underneath—demonstrates the use of extraneous wording:

> "*Unstructured book reviews that are found in most other websites often become too biased towards the reviewer's personal thought process. Such reviews hold very less value for the reader who is looking for an unbiased critical approach to the literary text.*"

> "Unstructured book reviews ~~that are found in most~~ found on other websites [are] often ~~become too~~ biased towards the reviewer's ~~personal~~ thought process[es]. Such reviews hold ~~very less~~ [minimal] value for ~~the~~ [a] reader ~~who is looking for~~ [seeking] an unbiased, critical approach to ~~the~~ a literary text."

> (Unstructured book reviews found on other websites are often biased towards the reviewer's personal thought processes. Such reviews hold minimal value for a reader seeking an unbiased, critical approach to a literary text.)

In this example, the modifiers "often" and "such" are necessary. Otherwise, the message these sentences would impart is that all book reviews on other websites are biased and of minimal value. Note the modifiers "most", "too", "very", and "less" are eliminated. The phrases "that are found in most" and "who is looking for" are reworded for succinct clarity.

Extraneous phrases are similar to the following:

Due to the face	Not only this
In order to	This, in turn,
Many a time	

Inclusion of extraneous modifiers and phrases dilutes your prose, and your writing lacks sophistication. This contributes to an overall impression of amateurish writing and inadequate expertise.

This may be my own anathema, but, when I see the words "get" or "got", I immediately think, "Amateur writer." "Get" and "got" are perfectly acceptable in spoken language, but, in my opinion, do not belong in professionally written web content.

I strongly recommend you subscribe to Daily Writing Tips. Excellent articles are sent daily by email on all aspects of writing. One daily writing tip I received was a list of synonyms for "give" (http://www.dailywritingtips.com/50-synonyms-and-idioms-for-give/). This should take care of the "gets" and "gots".

A thesaurus is an absolute must. I recommend Wordsmyth. It is, by far, the best online thesaurus I have found. And it is free.

Your hard work at developing your writing skills will pay off in spades, with client satisfaction, better projects, and higher remuneration. Almost makes grammar attractive, does it not?

Quick Summary
- An excellent writer needs cognitive, mechanical, and stylistic skills
- Solid basic grammar knowledge is imperative

- Resource books for grammar, spelling, and punctuation are invaluable
- Keep a thesaurus handy
- Eradicate extraneous words and phrases
- Your skills develop naturally as you write

Now we have grammar out of the way, we are ready to delve into your expertise. Perhaps you believe you have no expertise. Wrong. In the next chapter, I show you why and how you are an expert in diverse areas.

CHAPTER 6
YOU ARE AN EXPERT. REALLY.

"To know That which lies before us in daily life, Is the prime wisdom."
~ John Milton, Paradise Lost, 1667

I am about to demonstrate you are a whole lot smarter than you think. You are going to think about your life experiences in a completely different manner. Why? Because your personal and professional achievements and, yes, even your tribulations, are worth money.

It does not matter what life event you experience. It can be good or not-so-good. With personal insight, you learn new knowledge, tactics, or opinions regarding that particular life event.

I want to emphasize you do not need formal education or even practical experience to become an expert. A sincere curiosity, genuine interest and desire to write about a certain subject is all that is required.

To help you brainstorm about your possible areas of expertise, the following is a general list of topics:

Employment
- What jobs have you held?
- What positions within those occupations?
- Did or do you belong to a profession (i.e. teacher,

lawyer, accountant, financial advisor, etc.)?
- Are you certified at a skilled trade?
- Are you or have you been an owner/operator?
- Do you have management, supervisory, administration, and/or customer service representative experience?
- What were your duties as detailed in your job description?
- What industry did you work in?

Personal

What is your marital status? I know this seems rather personal, but I ask for a reason. There are clients seeking content regarding marital relationships, single life, how to survive a divorce, single parents, and grieving the loss of a spouse. Some of this might be too painful for you to consider writing about, but it is something to keep in mind if you feel capable of producing content on these topics.

Parenting

- This is a huge subject with several sub-focus opportunities. A point to remember – however old your children are, you have an equal number of years expertise.
- Sub-focus topics include: newborns; infants; toddlers; tweens; teens; and adult-child relationships. All these sub-focus topics can be broken down into small increments. A few examples are: bringing home your newborn or your child's first day of school.
- Are you a step-parent? What challenges have you overcome? Have there been situations where you were unable to resolve issues. Think about how you approached step-parenting. What techniques

helped and which were fruitless? With today's blended family society, this is a major market.

Caregiver

- Are you a caregiver to a child, spouse, or elderly parent?
- How do you cope with the physical aspects of caring for another?
- How do you manage your stress levels?
- Do you utilize respite care? What do you know about respite care? If you have received respite, what did you do to rejuvenate your energy during that time?
- Do you have self-care advice for caregivers?

Elderly Parents

- Baby Boomers are in the unique position of being the first generation raising children or paying for their college/university education and caring for elderly parents at the same time. Parents are starting families later in life, and seniors are living longer with advanced medical technology and better lifestyle opportunities. I predict the demand for content aimed at adult children caring for their senior parents will sharply increase in the coming years.

I volunteered at a seniors' recreation centre for a decade. I can state with assurance "80" is now the new "65". A generation ago, seniors retired at 65 and typically had a lifespan of 75 years. I have witnessed countless seniors both physically and socially active into their 90s. Seniors are devoted readers of senior life content.

Unfortunately, when a senior's health begins to decline, it often progresses at a rapid rate. This takes both the senior and their adult children by surprise in many cases. This opens the door for content dedicated to how to prepare for this eventuality.

Medical Conditions

- Is someone close to you or are you suffering from medical conditions?
- Do you have an interest in health issues? If so, in either case, there is great demand for web content based on providing consumers with up-to-date information.

Education

- Have you attended post-secondary education at a college or university? There is amazing potential in this expertise for articles on certification or degrees in every imaginable discipline. There are numerous clients seeking content detailing every known occupation.

Pets

- Do you own a cat, dog or other pet? Presto, you are an expert.

Hobbies and Interests

- If you have interests in various home hobbies, you can write web content based on virtually every hobby or interest.

To detail an accurate idea of how life experience or a true, abiding interest is invaluable, I will use my own career as an example.

I was a legal assistant for 20 years prior to freelance writing. This immediately opened doors for me to write legal-based web content. Although I was a legal assistant in Canada, all of my legal clients are based in the United States. I have written hundreds of legal information articles for lawyers directed at laypeople. I research state and federal law to ensure my content is accurate and for fodder to include in my articles.

I then won a project writing four articles for a client about a specific type of career and the education required for that occupation. I find this particularly interesting, and I pursue projects of this nature. This is a popular topic in continuous demand.

Although I do not have a background in health, this was another topic in which I am interested. After I won a project in this field, I had samples to prove I was a competent writer on health subjects. Besides other clients, I worked for an independent medical tourism client writing their web content about diagnoses, treatments, and prognoses.

I was asked by one of my law connections to ghostwrite eBooks about dogs and cats. This was an off-shoot from the regular legal work I wrote for this client. Another client asked me for fifty articles about wildlife in the Rockies. I did not know anything about wildlife, but I learned a lot during the process of research and writing. That project turned out to be one of my all-time favourite assignments.

I was in the process of being certified as a claims adjuster when I was forced by health issues to abandon both my educational and professional pursuits. My time in insurance classes was not wasted. Once again, I have written hundreds of insurance articles.

You can claim expertise in any area you choose. You do not have to possess a degree in that area. Life experiences are just as valuable.

I recommend you identify four or five specialty focusses. This gives you diversity, but does not stretch you too far. If you try to claim expertise in numerous fields, you will spend an inordinate, unprofitable amount of time on research. By concentrating on the four or five topics, you accumulate a wealth of knowledge and a list of credible sources of research information.

Quick Summary
- You do not need higher education to claim an expertise
- Your professional and life experience are equally valuable as expertise
- A sincere interest in a topic qualifies you as an expert
- Four or five areas of expertise are optimal

Did I say research? Guess what the next chapter contains...

CHAPTER 7
RESEARCH—IT IS EASIER THAN IT SEEMS

"You Could Look It Up."
~ James Thurber, story title,The Saturday Evening Post,
1941

Imagine you have won your first project. Once the exhilaration wears off, you might find yourself a little terrified. Where are you going to find enough material to write ten articles about the topic assigned? That was always my fear in the beginning—how on earth was I going to come up with ten different subtopics about motorcycle insurance and write 500 words on each? It is called "research". Research can be tricky. You might enter keywords into your Google search and come up with, well, not much. Panic sets in. This chapter is going to save you the angst I felt as a rookie.

Keywords

Research is all about *keywords* used in search engines. *Keywords* are words that are specifically relevant to the topic you are researching. *Keywords* are how you find information—research—for your topic. For instance, I Googled "what is a keyword" and received 301,000,000 results. At the top of the results was this definition: An informative word used in an information retrieval system to indicate the content of a document.

I recommend you use the latest, fastest, and most reliable search engines available, which are Google Chrome and Firefox (at the time of writing this book). As technology advances at an amazing rate, there may be a newer version of a search engine available when you are reading this section. One caveat to remember: new does not always mean better. It is worthwhile to investigate which search engine fulfills your needs.   Research is the foundation of excellent articles. You cannot write authoritative articles without grounded facts. Your goal is to provide your client with informative, factual, well-written articles.   *Keywords* and *phrases* that might seem obvious to you may not resonate as well with Internet research. Sometimes, it takes playing around to hit pay dirt. One method is to enter nouns and objects as *keywords*. Avoid using conjunctions and pronouns.

Phrases Method

Another strategy is to use *phrases*. To obtain *phrases* you need to ask a question. The best questions start with: "How do I…"   "Where is the…"   "What is the…" "What is a…" "What kind of…" "Who is…" "When was…" and watch the suggestions Google offers. The suggestions are the *phrases* you are seeking.

After the initial two or three question words you have entered, slowly add another word and look at the new suggestions. Keep adding one word at a time until you feel you have found the best *phrase* to work with.   As an example, I search for a new puppy that meets my criteria: mid-size; friendly; mid-energy; and, non-allergenic.   I begin with "what kind of":

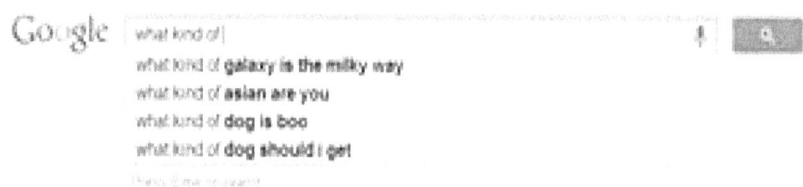

Google has already sent me in the right direction with the last *phrase*, but it is not exactly what I want. I add "puppy":

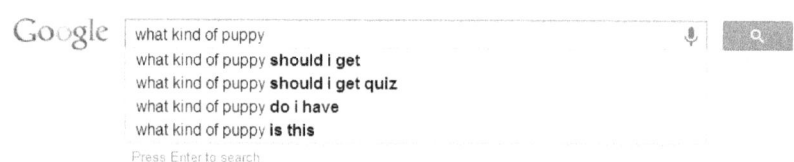

Not bad. I could take a quiz and, perhaps, find suggestions for an appropriate puppy. Let us take it further by adding "mid-size" and see what happens:

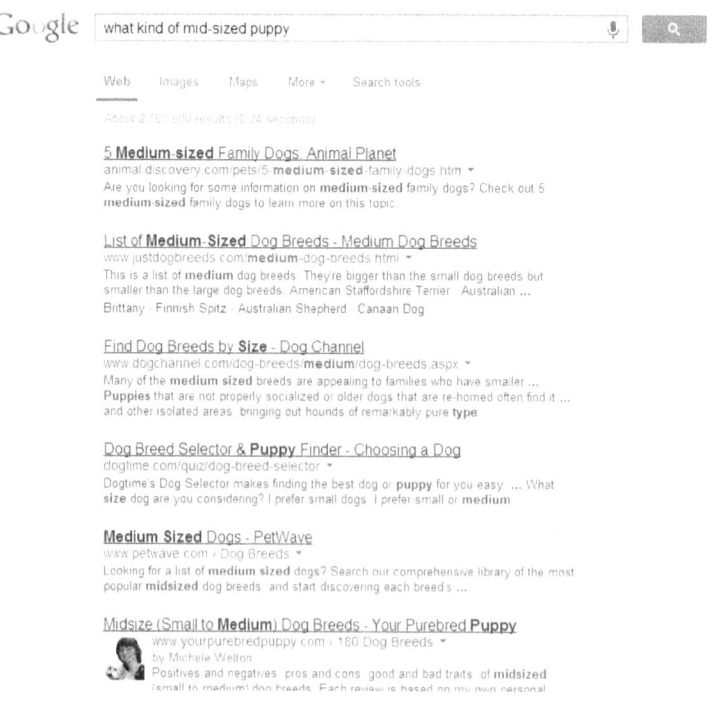

I received a sizeable return of 2,800,000 results with a few possibilities. I really need a non-allergenic puppy though.

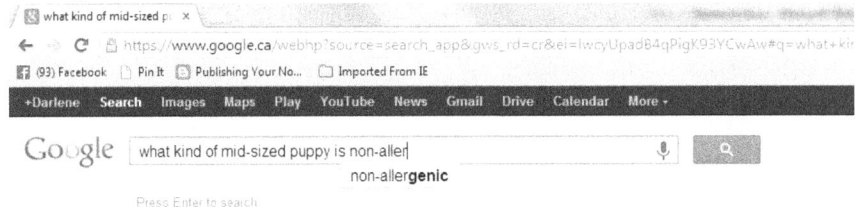

Google Chrome anticipated the rest of my question. Now, I click on the suggestion.

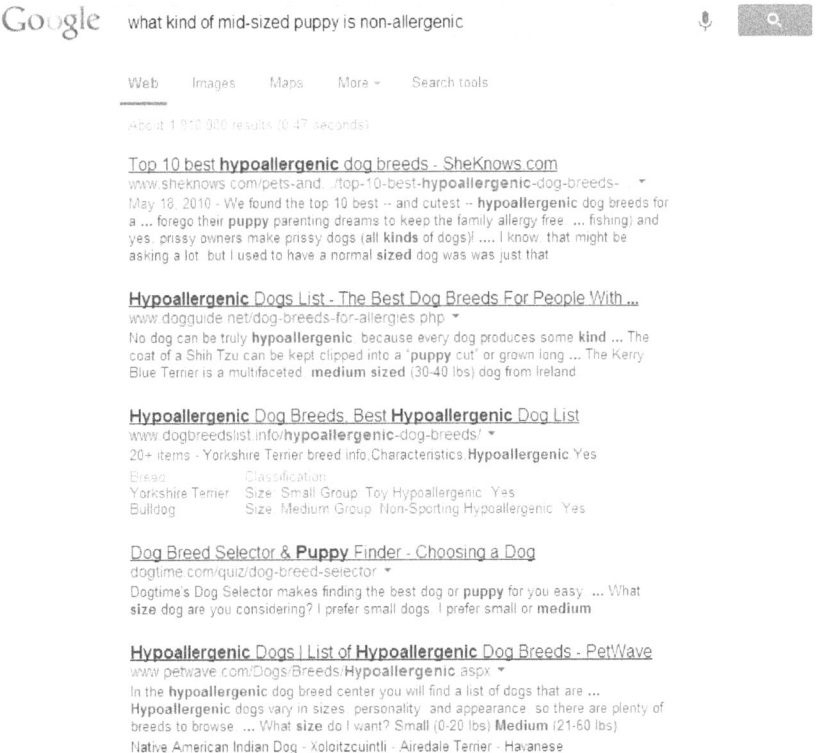

I have 1,910,000 results in 0.47 seconds. One of the search results is a list of hypoallergenic dogs. Hmmm. This sounds like it might be quite informative. It is. PetWave has an alphabetical list of hypoallergenic dogs. All I have to do now is click on a breed name and discover if a complete description of the breed's size, disposition, and energy level is provided.   Portuguese water dog sounds intriguing:

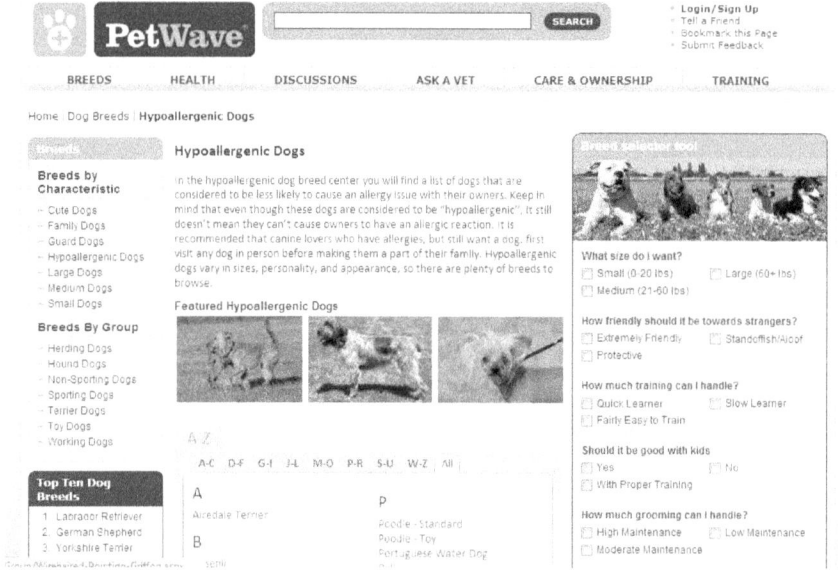

Everything I need is right here: introduction; history and health; temperament and personality; appearance and grooming; and, additional pictures. He is rather adorable! The entire search, if you add up the time results, took 0.71 seconds. The beauty of phrases is they can also give you additional ideas for content topics.

Boolean Operators

Another method is using what is called *Boolean operators*. *Boolean operators* are *keywords* you connect with the words "and", "or", or "and not". The first two connectors are used to search for specific topics. The "and not" eliminates any topics you are not interested in. It is important to remember to always capitalize your *Boolean operators*. I try for a puppy again using *Boolean operators*:

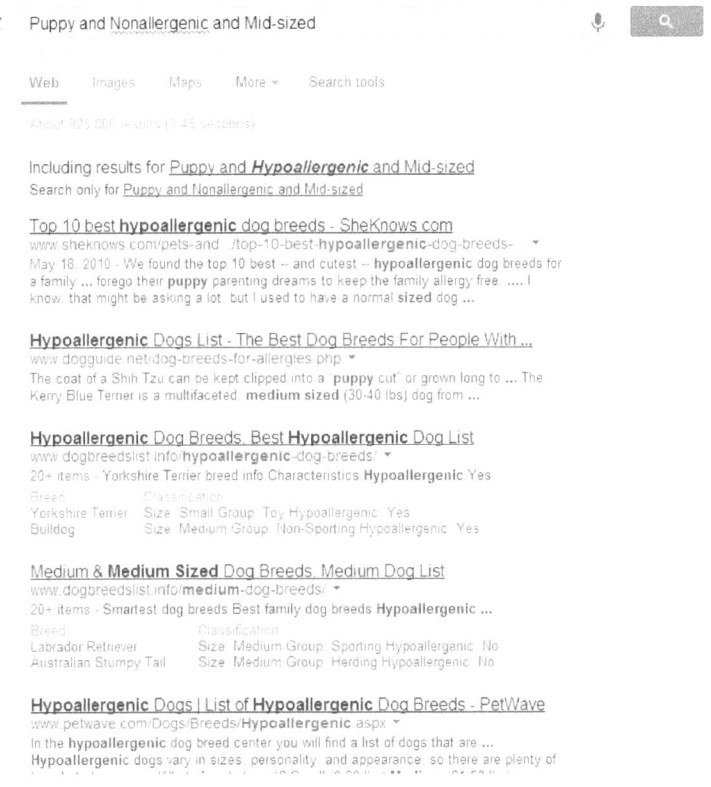

I typed in "Puppy and Non-allergenic and Mid-sized". In 0.46 seconds I received a more specific list, including the website I visited earlier. *Boolean operators* are powerful tools. Try to use them as much as possible if you know the precise information you need. *Boolean operators* will not assist you if you are seeking topic ideas via Google suggestions. *Boolean operators* are a restrictive form of research.

Google Scholar

A neat trick to accessing references is to search Google Scholar. The results often only provide abstracts, but if you click on "Cited by" or "Related articles" you find leads to more articles. To receive up-to-date references, notice on the left side bar there is a section entitled "Any Time". Click on an appropriate date and you receive only articles written since that time. Google Scholar sorts results according to relevance, rather than latest date.

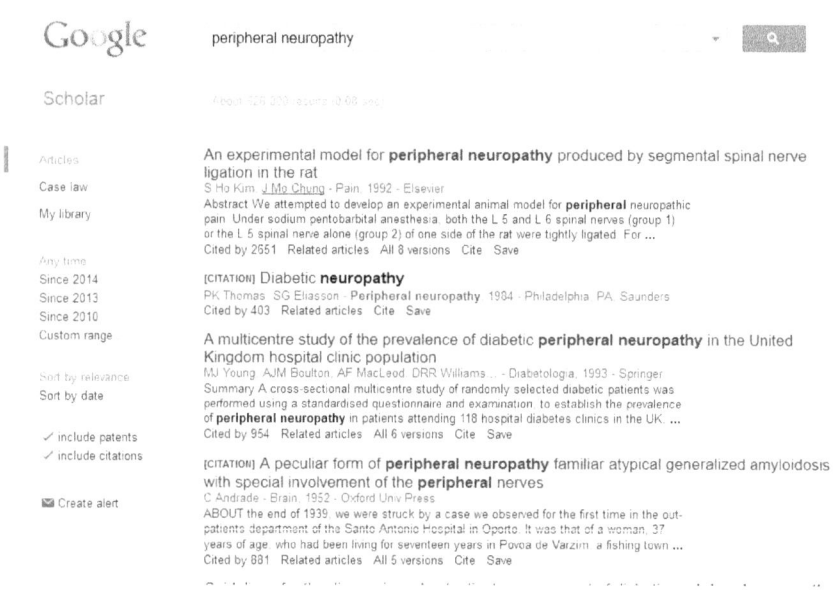

Types of Research

There are two types of research: *hard* and *soft*. *Hard research* is of a scientific nature. It is hard core facts and figures. It does not contain opinions, only datum. *Hard research* contains facts, statistics, objectives that can be measured. In other words, the evidence cannot be disproven. It is unlikely you will write this type of content, unless you have academic clients. The percentage of academic clients is quite low.

Should you require *hard research*, Google Scholar is your best option.

Soft research is the most common type of project

posted. This is subjective, rather than objective as in *hard research*. It cannot be measured. *Soft research* is based on opinions and culture-based. You do not need to include data. My puppy search is an example of *soft research*.

Resources suitable for *soft research* are listed in the next section. Research Resources For every topic, you should have at least three different credible resources. You will find, in some cases, your research results in more than one opinion on your topic. This is where the credibility of your resources comes into play. If two of three resources have the same opinion, use your common sense and good judgment to elect whether to follow those opinions. If the opinion does not make logical sense, even though two of three resources have stated it, dig deeper. I used a crucial word in the above paragraph: *credible*. I cannot emphasize enough the magnitude of this single word. As I mentioned earlier, the credibility of your written content depends solely on excellent research skills. Credible resources are:

- Government websites, professional associations relevant to your topic (i.e. American Association of Engineers, American Society of Civil Engineers), and university websites
- Health organizations such as Mayo Clinic, WebMD, Cancer.org, CDC.gov, and PubMed are credible
- Scientific websites include Discovery.com, Nature.com, ScientificAmerican.com, NASA.gov, ScienceDaily.com, and The-Scientist.com
- Parenting websites that may be helpful are BabyCenter.com and Parenting.com.
- ConsumerReports.org and Forbes.com are two reliable starting points for consumer affairs.
- Current events are at NPR.org and Time.Com.
- Smithsonian.com is a fascinating source of information
- Home and garden sites BHG.com and

MarthaStewart.com have a plethora of information
- For fur and feather babies, try PawNation.com, petMD.com, and WebVet.com.

Credible resources vary with your project description.

Never, ever, use Wikipedia articles as a primary resource. However, scroll to the bottom of the entry to references used by Wikipedia. This might lead to authentic information.

"Joe Blow's" blog about engineering is not a credible resource. Blogs, web content on company sites, and articles on sites, such as Ezines, are not legitimate resources. Anyone can write an article with incorrect information and proclaim themselves an expert. Do your due diligence when researching and ensure your information is factual and written by a bona fide expert.

How to Reduce Your Research Time

Say your client has requested twenty interior design articles. The fastest, most efficient method of researching and writing the twenty articles is to complete your research on all twenty subtopics prior to writing the articles. If you research one subtopic at time and write each individual article, you are wasting valuable time. You are, in effect, "double-doing" your research.

Organize your three credible resources on each subtopic with a paperclip and write one article after another until you have worked your way through your research pile. I promise, this saves you hours. When you are working a *fixed price* project, hours spent determines whether you make or lose money on that project. On an overall note, research is a learned skill and it may be slow in the beginning. However, as time goes on and you perfect your research skills, it is completed faster and easier than you believed possible.

Using the best approach to research, understanding the type of information required, knowledge of credible resources, and practice enables you to provide your client with excellent content. The likelihood the client leaves a positive recommendation and hires you for further projects increases immeasurably (this sentence is the result of *hard research*).

Quick Summary

Relevant *keywords* are essential to research. Research is the foundation of factual, well-written content Keyword *phrases* is a method of research and garnering content ideas *Boolean operators* are powerful tools for narrowing research topics There are two types of research: *hard* and *soft* Credible research resources must be utilized for accurate information Research time can be reduced by conducting all your research in one session

On to the next chapter where we explore adding another arsenal to writing fabulous content: Search Engine Optimization, commonly referred to as SEO.

CHAPTER 8
SEARCH ENGINE OPTIMIZATION DEMYSTIFIED

"The mind of man is capable of anything—because everything is in it, all the past as well as all the future."
~ Joseph Conrad, Heart of Darkness, 1902

"SEO articles" is a phrase commonly seen in job descriptions. Search Engine Optimization is frequently known by the acronym "SEO". For example, the job description may say:

"I need a full-time writer who can write SEO articles for me. Keywords are to appear in the 1st and 3rd paragraph" First of all, the most important thing to remember is to write excellent content that is topically relevant, tightly written, informative, and engaging. Google recently made two major updates to its algorithms. Google's search engines bypass a SEO-laden article. A well-written piece of work ranks higher than before the updates. No doubt, search engines will continue to update algorithms on a regular basis. SEO is not difficult to master. There is considerable debate whether SEO is effective, but many clients still believe it is. And you are here to make clients happy. Right?

What is SEO?

SEO, in a nutshell, is *keywords* or *phrases* relevant to

the subject matter of the article, with specific words or phrases inserted at precise locations within the article. These *keywords* or *phrases* must be written seamlessly into the article, so they do not appear evident. They typically appear in:

- The title
- Subtitles
- The first paragraph
- The last paragraph

SEO Density

Another frequent request from a client is SEO *density*. This simply means the percentage of the article that contains the *keywords*. An example: A client requests two percent *keyword density* in a 100 word article. The *keywords* in this case would appear two times. A 500 word article at two percent *density* includes the *keywords* ten times. Optimum *keyword density* is one to three percent. Anything over three percent is known as "keyword-stuffing". It is ineffective and search engines ignore it. I guarantee there will be instances where the client wants a five percent or greater *keyword density* in the article. Do not argue. And do not sweat the small stuff. If that is what the client requests, give the client what they want.

I wrote thirty articles for a Melbourne, Australian chiropractor. He wanted five percent *density* with the *keywords* "Melbourne Chiropractor". That is what I wrote and received payment for. Then he asked for another thirty articles with the *keywords* "Chiropractor Melbourne" at five percent *density*. I messaged him to explain it is impossible to write anything logical with the second set of *keywords*. They would be prominent, rather than melding into the articles, and the articles would appear keyword-stuffed. He was adamant. So, that is what I wrote and received payment for.

The moral of the story is you are paid to produce exactly what the client expects. The old adage "The customer is always right." applies. Even though you know the project is going to read like junk, you are paid to write it, not to worry about whether it drives traffic to the client's site. That is their problem, not yours. Your name does not appear as a byline. Just do not use such an article in your portfolio!

How Do I Know Which Keywords to Use?

Before you panic wondering how on earth you are going to figure out what *keywords* to use, relax. The client almost always tells you what *keywords* to use and where to place them.   In the rare case a client does not inform you of the *keywords* or placement, an elementary exercise is to take up paper and pencil and brainstorm keywords you think you would use to search for the particular topic you are assigned. You can also use the free online Google Keyword Planner tool to assist you if you are having difficulties brainstorming.

Then simply type them into a search engine and see what pops up. If your *keywords* are confirmed by your research, you are off to the races.

Phrases or Long Tail Keywords

Phrases are most often referred to as *long tail keywords*. As a demonstration, let us look at the following project description:

> *"I'm in need of someone to write blogs about: - Parenting - Education - COPPA (Children Online Privacy Protection Act) - Technology (Devices and applications). The above topics should be centered around the family and focused on parents with kids aged 4-12. The tone should be*

fun and light. I will also need a list of 90 one liner tips around the 4 topics for social media purposes. I will first ask you for the list of tips - and a blog sample (both paid). If they're well written and satisfactory then I will need blogs every week."

The client has not asked for SEO articles, but, for the sake of this exercise, we are going to search for *long tail keywords*. This is similar to the searches we conducted in Chapter 7.

As the client has not been specific about the "Technology (Devices and applications) topic (which you would query to learn exactly what is meant), we will use the parenting category. Remember, you need a blog article and about 23 one line tips for each topic.

I type in parenting advice:

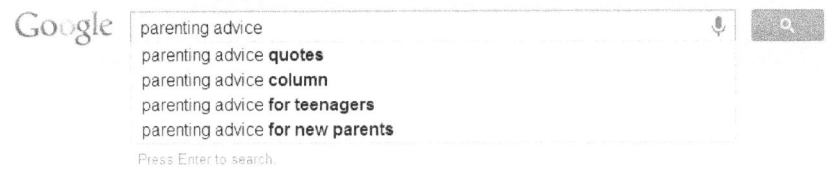

My search results come up with four possibilities: quotes; column; for teenagers; and, for new parents. The first two of the four phrases could be relevant, especially for the one-liners. Then, I take it a little further to be more specific. I add the words "for parents of".

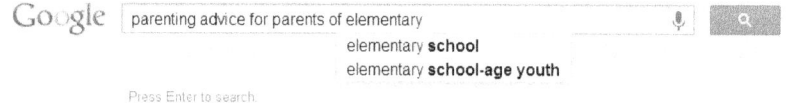

Now you can see *long tail keywords* appear:
- Parenting advice for parents of preschoolers
- Parenting tips for parents of teenagers.

Now we modify the search to eliminate "preschoolers" and "teenagers" and substitute "elementary".

Our results give us: Parenting advice for parents of elementary school Parenting advice for parents of elementary school-age youth. As you can see, I did not get past the word "elementary" before two suggestions appeared. All of these *phrases* are *long tail keywords* that can be incorporated into an SEO article. *Long tail keywords* consisting of 11 to 25 characters are best. Technically minded people can get quite in-depth and complicated about SEO *keywords*. It is really not necessary as a freelance writer to delve too deeply into the subject. A word of caution: do not get sucked in by software vendors that promise you the world, or at least the best *keyword* research software in the world. You do not need software! Do not waste your money.

To cap this chapter off, SEO means "search engine optimization". It is not a scary, insurmountable obstacle. Ninety-five percent of the time, the client tells you what *keywords* to use and where to place them in the articles. Seldom does the client not provide this information. In that case, using the simple examples demonstrated above supplies you with *keywords* and *long tail keywords*. It really is that easy.

Quick Summary

SEO means "search engine optimization" SEO are relevant *keywords* or *phrases* search engines recognize *Keywords* are strategically placed seamlessly into content SEO *density* is the number of times a *keyword* appears in content translated into a percentage *Keywords* are usually provided by clients Google Keyword Planner is helpful for identifying *keywords* *Phrases* or *long tail keywords* between 11 to 25 characters are ideal When you turn the page, we finally get into the great stuff—writing for the web. You are well prepared and, I hope, eager to test your writing capabilities.

CHAPTER 9
WRITING WEB CONTENT—FORGET (SOME OF) WHAT YOUR ENGLISHTEACHER TAUGHT

"Style is the dress of thoughts;"
~ *Samuel Wesley, 1700*

Writing web content is a completely different beast. You may have writing experience as an author or journalist or through personal journaling or your day job. When it comes to writing web content, you need to learn a different set of rules. A certain amount of articles written for clients are intended for their blogs; therefore, if you are a blogger, you may have a leg up already.

Times New Roman 12 is the most common, and best, font for articles.

Readability

Writing for the web is all about *readability*. Sounds like a redundant piece of advice, but not really. The average reading level of a consumer is Grade 8. Some consumers are at a much lower level—Grade 3. Shocking, perhaps, but true. In Microsoft Word, click on "Spelling and Grammar" in the "Proofing" section. Click "Options". Underneath the subtitle "When checking spelling and grammar in Word", tick the box for "Show readability statistics". It shows statistics for counts (words, characters, paragraphs, and sentences), averages, and readability. I tested *readability* for this book, and the "Averages" and "Readability" statistics are: Averages Sentences per paragraph 2.5 Words per sentence 14.6 Characters per word 4.8 Readability Passive sentences 12% Flesch Reading Ease 62.7 Flesch-Kincaid Grade Level 7.6

The general consensus is you should aim between the 60 and 70 percent reading ease range. Reading ease scores are heavily influenced by how many words are in a sentence, and how many sentences are in a paragraph. Shorter and fewer sentences in paragraphs increases the reading ease score considerably.

For a complete list of online content *readability* tests and a deeper understanding of readability click here. This is an excellent blog post by Raven Internet Marketing Tools listing the pros and cons of various *readability* tests.

Skimmers

An article has ten seconds to grab a reader's attention. That is it. If your title and first few sentences do not resonate, you have lost your audience. If you do tempt the reader further, they will not read word-for-word. Readers skim on the Internet and absorb approximately 20 percent of what they read. That means 80 percent of your article is not read, unless it is captivating, informative, and engaging as to completely draw in the reader's interest. You might wonder how you are going to present your articles so they are actually read. There are methods of writing and formatting an article to counteract these drawbacks.

Be Active

Active language wins hands-down over passive wording. It provides extra panache you need to keep your prose engaging. Root out all the "to be", "had been", "will be", "will have", "will have been", "would be", "is going to be", "should be", and "should have been" phrases and rewrite the sentence. A passive sentence vs. an active one: "The students will have been told their marks by next Friday." (passive) "The students receive their marks next Friday." (active) Tight prose is a marker of a great freelance writer. Be ruthless and eliminate passive language. Your client will thank you by requesting your services again.

Word Choices

Place strong word choices at the beginning and end of sentences. This means using nouns and verbs as much as possible, and adjectives and adverbs sparingly.

Keep the language simple. Utilize words in common usage. If there are complex variations of a word, with the exact same meaning, use the less sophisticated word. Web content is not meant to be written in a literary fashion; it is intended to provide useful information for the average person.

Be clear and concise with your wording to avoid ambiguity. Way back in college, our instructor gave us extra points if we looked up the meaning of "ambiguity" during our break and returned with the correct answer. It is a good word never to forget.

If possible, do not use jargon or acronyms. Sometimes, however, it is impossible to avoid including jargon and acronyms, depending on the subject matter. If you must include them, give a brief explanation of the meaning of the lingo or complete name associated with the acronym the first time it appears in the article.

Keep a thesaurus at hand or, as previously mentioned, use an online tool, such as Wordsmyth. Watch for word repetition, a nemesis for all writers. We all have certain thought processes and, unconsciously, have favorite words. My rule of thumb is do not repeat the same descriptive word more than once every 500 words. Never include a word if you are not sure of its meaning.

I edited a novel for a fantastic author who attempted to elevate the sophistication of her writing with complex words. Unfortunately, she misused these words. The result was her sentences as written were incomprehensible or the meaning was negatively altered.

The moral of the story: Look it up in the dictionary!

Stylistic Considerations

Writing web content means forgetting some of what your English teacher drilled into your head. Information needs to be presented in a stylistic manner suitable for skimmers. The following is a general guide for numerals, capitalization, abbreviations, and punctuation. If you are not sure how to treat a name, word, or number, Google the term for a definitive answer or consult *The Chicago Manual of Style*.

Numerals:

- Spell out numbers below nine; use figures for 10 and above.
- Use figures for ages, dates, money, percentages, days of the month, temperatures, etc. Spell out a figure when it begins a sentence. Better yet, rephrase your sentence to avoid the number placed as the first word.
- Abbreviate numbers when appropriate—2.3 billion instead of 2,300,000,000.
- Keep monetary figures simple—$125 instead of $125.00.
- The time of day should read 3 pm rather than 3:00 pm. Periods are not necessary for "pm" and "am".

They can be written in SMALL CAPITALS or lowercase.
- Spell out simple fractions—three-quarters. Use numerals when a whole number is accompanied by a fraction—5¾.
- Do not use Roman numerals unless they are explicitly associated with a name—World War II.

Capitalization:
- Capitalize all proper nouns.
- If a person is designated a specific title, capitalize the title if it is before the person's name. If the title follows the person's name, do not capitalize— Principal John Doe; John Doe, principal of Mission Secondary School. Occupations placed before a person's name are not capitalized.
- Capitalize the United States or United Nations only if they are nouns.
- Capitalize all foreign countries and all nationalities.
- Capitalize religious or spiritual denominations.
- Capitalize historic events—the Gulf War—and special occasions—Thanksgiving.
- Capitalize all astronomy descriptions—Milky Way. Do not capitalize "earth" unless it is used in conjunction with other capitalized celestial bodies—"Where on earth did he go?" or "The distance from Earth to Jupiter is 545.6 million miles."
- Capitalize the names of streets, highways, etc.
- Do not capitalize compass points—The cabin is north of Dunn Burying Ground—but capitalize specific regions—in the Pacific Northwest.

Abbreviations:
- A state can be abbreviated only if it is preceded by

a location within that state—Seattle, WA.

- Weights and measures can be abbreviated. Do not put a period at the end of the abbreviation.

Punctuation:

- Do not indent the first line of paragraphs unless instructed by your client.
- One space after a period. The two space rule is passé in this digital age.
- No period after salutatory designations — Mr, Mrs, Ms, Dr, Rev
- Serial commas are a matter of great debate. Whether you choose to use them or not is a personal choice or may be dictated by the client. I, personally, prefer the use of serial commas as they eliminate possible ambiguities. Serial commas are popular in North America. The United Kingdom and Europe seldom employ serial commas.
- If you are writing about the 1980s, there is no apostrophe between the "0" and "s".
- In a double-subject possessive situation, the apostrophe is placed after the second subject— John and Mary's baby is a boy.
- Place a comma before a conjunction. A little trick to decide whether a comma is required is to take the conjunction word out and, if there are two complete sentences, include the comma.
- Closing punctuation is always within quotation marks. Dates are written month, day, and year— May 1, 2011. Do not add "st", "nd", "rd", or "th" to the day.

Bulleted Lists

Bulleted lists are a writer's best friend. You may notice I use them frequently. Lists are concise, bite-sized chunks of information that are easily comprehensible, rather than laying out items in sentences. However, do not write an entire article with bulleted lists.

Lists should consist of the same syntax, either sentence fragments or full sentences. The two should not be mixed together in the same list. If you are using full sentences in your list, include closing punctuation at the end of each bulleted point. Omit closing punctuation for sentence fragments.

Tone

Write articles in a casual, yet professional, manner. Write as if you are talking with the reader and explaining what your article is conveying.

Almost always write from a second person point-of-view. You want the article to speak directly to the reader. Use the words "you" and "your".

This book is written from the second person point-of-view. I am talking directly to you, in a conversational tone, about a professional occupation.

Title

Keep the length of your title short. The optimum number of words is seven. The title should not exceed ten words. Ensure the title is relevant to the content of the article. Nothing is more frustrating than clicking on a title to discover the article content is almost completely irrelevant. If your title is "How to Make Apple Cider", your article must be devoted to that subject alone. Adding snippets of information about using extra apples to make a pie does not belong in that specific article.

Introductory Paragraph

My book mentor introduced me to a saying: "Tell them what you are going to tell them, and then tell them again."

The purpose of the introductory paragraph is to fulfill the first part of this advice. Two or three short sentences should suffice. Watch for redundancies. With the exception of the above advice, ensure you are not stating a point and then repeating it again with different phrasing.

If your article is about how to grow carrots, state your article is about how to grow carrots, the perfect soil for growing carrots, preventing pests from destroying the carrots, and harvest time.

Subsections

Break your article into as many subsections as is reasonable. From the above introductory paragraph, you can have:

- Varieties of carrots
- Balancing Soil
- Methods of Preventing Pests
- Harvest Time in Various
- Climate Zones

You want to have meaningful subtitles to enable the reader to instantly understand what the subsection information contains.

Start your subsection with pertinent, declarative, preliminary information. Only one paragraph per idea (i.e. There are x number of carrot varieties.) Follow up with two or three sentences explaining your preliminary statement. Keep the sentences short, but of varying lengths.

Repeat subsections until you have written all of the information you intend to provide the reader.

Underline or bold each subtitle section.

After the final subsection, you want to "tell them again." Summarize the pivotal facts in a few sentences.

White Space

Your job is to fill white space with black letters. You

must also present what you have written in a style that accommodates the web content reader.

We have talked about how to write to satisfy readers, but there is one last thing that makes all the difference. White space. By that, I mean have lots of white space between your title, subtitles, subsections, and summary. Add an extra return in these areas, and you instantly notice the article is not cramped.

Stuck On Where to Start?

There is no rule an article must be written consecutively. If you have trouble with the introduction, skip it for the time being. Work on subsections. You do not need to write these in order, either.

As you fill in your article, the introduction becomes easier to formulate.

Quick Summary

- Use Times New Roman 12 font
- The average reading level of a consumer is Grade 8
- Web content readers are skimmers, reading only twenty percent of an article
- Use active language
- Use simple rather than complex versions of words
- A thesaurus is a must
- Ensure numerals, capitalization, abbreviations and punctuation are in accordance with the *Chicago Manual of Style*
- Bulleted lists are an excellent choice for readability
- Write in second person point-of-view
- Title must be relevant to the content and no longer than ten words
- Break articles into an introductory paragraph, subsections, and a summary

- Include white space
- Articles do not have to be written consecutively

Web Content Sample (written for an encyclopedia entry)

Dutch Language

The Dutch language is also known as Netherlandic or Nederlands. Dutch belongs to the Low Franconian group of the West Germanic languages. Afrikaans, amongst many other languages, is derived from Dutch.

Dutch, the official language of the Netherlands and Suriname, a former Dutch colony, is spoken by approximately 27 million people. The name "Dutch" originates from the ancestor of Germanic languages, Proto-Germanic.

Old Dutch (c450-c1150)

Dutch is descended from Old Frankish. Its evolution began with the Second Germanic consonant shift. Not all Old Frankish dialects participated in the consonant shift, including Dutch. Old Frankish dialects that did not take part in consonant shift became known as Old Low Franconian and, thus, the appellation of Old Dutch was given. Old Low Franconian had two subgroups: East Low Franconian and West Low Franconian. Eventually Dutch became the dominant language, and East Low Franconian merged into West Low Franconian.

Aside from a few sentences, the only surviving written text from this period is a Book of Psalms translation.

Middle Dutch (c1150-c1500)

Written texts from the Middle Dutch period show there was no standard written Dutch. People wrote phonetically in their local dialects, which led to different pronunciations.

Spelling was irregular with words spelled in multiple ways, sometimes within the same text. During this time, the traditional Latin alphabet was used but it was unsuitable, as it did not contain enough letters for the Dutch language. Authors used personal choices, such as "c" versus "k", when spelling words.

Writers were faced with Dutch words with vowel and consonant sounds which were not addressed by the Latin alphabet. Long and short vowels were not differentiated at that time leading to confusion. Some authors duplicated vowels, while others added an "i" or "e".

In the 1200s, there was an attempt to establish a standard written form, which had limited success as texts continued to be written in local dialects.

Middle Dutch used a case system, but this was substantially phased out during this era.

Modern Dutch (c1500-present)

Written Modern Dutch emerged from the Flemish dialect. At the beginning of this era, Flanders and Brabant were culturally important and the Flemish dialect became prominent. Antwerp fell to the Spanish in 1585, and refugees fled north to Holland where the Flemish dialect entrenched itself.

A standard written version of Dutch was further established by a translation of the Scriptures between 1619 and 1637. Standard written Dutch and spelling spread along with distribution of the translation.

Since that time, grammar has been simplified and some pronunciations altered, but Dutch remains essentially unchanged.

Modern spoken standard Dutch differs from written Dutch. The vernacular is derived from dialects in the North, while the writing system is imported from the South. Written Dutch is more formal than spoken Dutch. Spoken Dutch still has many dialects used mainly by older citizens and in rural areas, while most towns and cities speak the official standard form.

Today the Dutch Language Union ("Nederlandse Taalunie"), established in 1980, seeks to standardize the Dutch language. The Union is not responsible for the language's regulation. The Union publishes the "Wordlist of the Dutch Language" with official spellings, but does not provide the meanings of words. It is popularly known as the Green Booklet, due to the color of the cover.

CHAPTER 10
REVIEW, EDIT AND PROOFREAD—THREE NON-NEGOTIABLES

"Nothing is more powerful than habit."
~ Ovid, The Art of Love, c. 2 BC

Fix the acronym REP in your mind. Review, Edit, and Proof. You are going to repeat this process for every piece of writing you produce. Always. So, you might as well establish good REP habits.

Review

A common thread in writing advice books and blogs is to block your internal editor while you are writing your article and let the writing flow. Great advice if you are able to do this. Personally, I cannot turn off the editor while I write. I no longer fight the losing battle. It is the way I naturally write.

If it is possible to ignore your editing voice and continuously write, certainly follow this strategy. If you are unable to silence that voice in your head, do not worry unnecessarily. Either way, you are doing the work you are hired to do.

Once you finish writing, spell and grammar check with MS Tools. Then, read over your work with special attention to the following:

- Spelling Punctuation
- Typographical errors
- Verb tense
- Phrase structure
- Sentence structure
- Repetitive words
- Excess wordiness
- Fact checking
- Consistent font Proper formatting

The next step is to print your article. I firmly take the stance you cannot thoroughly edit work on the screen. You locate errors on paper you miss on the screen. Have a red pen and ruler handy.

Read the article word by word, line by line. Place the ruler under each line. This method prevents your eyes from skipping up or down sentences. Read it aloud. This forces you to slow down rather than skim through. If you feel foolish reading it verbally (I did because I often had family members at home), move your lips with each word.

Edit

When you find an error—a typo, wrong word choice, incorrect punctuation, awkward phrasing, redundancy, excess wordiness, an inconsistency in the thread of the article—correct it with a red pen and draw a big circle around it. This ensures you do not miss corrections when you input your changes into the document on the computer.

Once you have completely read the draft and circled all mistakes, make the changes on your computer. Print off another copy of the article. Put the original marked-up copy and the newly printed copy side-by-side on your desk. Compare the two documents line by line, once again using your ruler. Make sure you catch all the editing changes you made on the first draft.

Proofread

Finally, have one more read through with an eye for proper flow of thoughts, ambiguities, layout (which we talked about in Chapter 9), and grammatical and typographical errors. This is your final phase of REP.

REP might sound like it is a lot of extra work. Many writers believe they can rely on autocorrect for spelling and grammar. These tools are helpful, but not perfect. This applies equally to software, such as Grammarly. Editors have tested editing software programs and, thus far, all of them are lacking. As an editor, I do not use software. This extra mile you put in is what earns you kudos from clients.

Feedback on your profile from clients complaining about editorial standards is definitely not something you want. Remember, although, you are not perfect. It is likely you will miss an error once in a while.

I followed this strategy religiously. Out of the thousands of articles I wrote, not one was rejected. That is what you want to aim for. I am not saying they were all 100 percent correct, but whatever errors existed must have been minor.

Going the extra mile with REP, no matter how busy you are, is essential. It is not a process you can skip and cross your fingers your work is error-free. I guarantee there will be more than one change required in every article you write. On paper, it is apparent to you what changes are required for the first draft to shape into the perfect completed article.

Plagiarism—The Death Knell

After you have read, edited, and proofread your article, the most important step follows: checking for plagiarism. You might feel offended I even bring the subject up because you would never plagiarize. The next paragraphs explain my reasons. Reading research materials might inadvertently lead to writing your article using identical phrases and/or words because they have stuck in your mind. It happens to us all. But, if you are caught plagiarizing, the bells begin to toll as your career plummets into the grave because you are permanently banned from the content broker's website. Under no circumstances is plagiarism tolerated.

Copyscape is a super, cheap solution to ensuring this never happens to you. Paste the text of your article into Copyscape's box, and Copyscape either pronounces the article clear or lists where plagiarism of content has occurred. Sometimes, you might have to monkey around with a few words to clear the article or make a judgment call if the words or phrases in question cannot be changed. For instance, the descriptions "United State of America", "USA", "US or "U.S." are impossible to avoid. In this case, it is acceptable to use any of the above.

It is the word-for-word alerts to which you need to pay special attention. In those cases, rewrite your sentences, grab your thesaurus for synonyms, and use your imagination. Freelance writers are often called upon to be "creative writers".

Quick Summary
- Follow the reviewing, editing, and proofreading process to provide quality, error-free work
- Never submit work without running it through a plagiarism tool

Practice rep and happy clients return to ask for more

work.

CHAPTER 11
HOW TO EARN MONEY WHILE BUILDING YOUR PORTFOLIO

"They can do all because they think they can"

~ Virgil, Aeneid, c 19 BC

It is now time to build your portfolio and earn money. You have read numerous chapters and copious amounts of information to reach this stage. I hope you are excited, because I am for you.

Theory is an essential background, but implementing those theoretical principles is time consuming for your first few articles. Please do not expect to whiz through your initial articles. It is going to take longer to refer back to previous chapters to create a piece of written art.

You may not realize this, but you possess all the tools required to earn money. You have:

- drilled down your expertise learned about SEO
- discovered methods of research
- gained insights about the principles of writing web content
- examined the components of delivering a well-crafted, edited, and proofread article

If necessary, go back and review those chapters before you write your article. Or, you can refer to them when your article is complete. Either way works. I now challenge you to write one article for each of your four chosen niches. At some point, you have to put the guidebook down and do the work. It is hard work. Writing is not an easy occupation as discussed in the beginning. The rewards although...

You are now writing for pay. Keep that in mind as you write these articles. This is the reason you bought this book. I have expended much time and energy to get you to this point. Now you are going to take over. From here on in, I merely guide you through various processes and strategies.

We are the most critical of our own words. Ping that self-doubt devil off your shoulder. Have confidence. Be assured you have the necessary tools to write a relevant, engaging, and interesting article and it will sell. I have no doubts whatsoever your articles will sell if you diligently apply the information contained in this book.

I suggest you browse through the writers' guidelines at the end of Chapter 13, Constant Content Overview, to ensure you are in compliance, because this is where you are going to sell your first articles that form your portfolio. So, begin writing your articles. When you have four of the best articles you have ever written, we will meet up again in the next three chapters where you create your profile, learn how to boost your profile, and submit your articles for sale.

Quick Summary

Assignment: Write four articles, polished and ready to sell I am still excited! How about you?

CHAPTER 12
CREATE A PROFILE THAT SPARKLES

"You Never Get a Second Chance to Make a First Impressions
~ Attribution Uncertain (Oscar Wilde; Will Rogers; Mark Twain)

When you commence your career as a freelance writer, droves of emails with project offers do not magically appear. That does not happen until you have established a fantastic profile, portfolio, and reputation. The first website on which you will create your profile is Constant Content. Constant Content is a content broker, and we discuss how it operates in greater detail in Chapter 13, Constant Content Overview.

When you walk into a new doctor's office your initial impression of the office is formed through the first person you meet, usually the receptionist. A relaxed, professional receptionist instantly puts you at ease. You have the feeling you are going to be comfortable in that office.

This analogy is true of freelance websites. Your profile is the first impression. You need to sell yourself and your amazing writing abilities. This is the only opportunity you have to make that first great impression.

How do you create a captivating profile? You need to include certain elements that answer any potential questions a client has. Your profile should anticipate a client's questions and put him or her at ease about your capabilities.

Personal Information

Inclusion of personal information—your website, email address, telephone number—may be permitted or forbidden. Ensure you are not in contravention of personal information inclusion rules on each income source.

Profile Picture

A professional profile picture is required. By professional, I mean a crisp head shot photograph that depicts you in a businesslike fashion. You do not need a professional photographer. Ask someone to take a number of pictures and select the one that shows you in the best possible light. The picture should be only from the shoulders up. No full body images. Please do not use an avatar, cartoonish caricature, or your pet as a profile picture. This screams amateurish. Lastly, say "cheese" and smile naturally!

Resume

The next element you work on is the "resume" portion of your profile. It might be all one section or divided into subsections. What you want to convey to potential clients is basically the same details as would be included in a formal resume. Your skills, relevant work history, education, certifications, and licenses. As an example, the following is one of my overviews (or Resume/C.V./):

"I am a Native English speaking fiction and nonfiction writer, blogger, reviewer and editor, who writes substantive, well-researched content in the medical, education, legal, insurance, and pet fields. These are topics for which I have great enthusiasm, and I welcome the opportunity to write quality content based on these niches.

I do not fill my content with fluff and filler words. Every word has meaning that adds to the project. I consider projects from an advocacy point of view. Each assignment, regardless of its nature, ultimately contains information that might assist people to enrich their daily lives or make informed decisions. This aspect is important to me.

Research is a passion. I follow leads to compile all relevant information and utilize no less than three reputable sources.

I am a professional. My work illustrates my high standards. I do my utmost to ensure grammatical errors, spelling mistakes, factual inaccuracies, and plagiarism never occurs."

Important Information Your Resume Imparts

This overview gives the client a lot of important information:

- I am a Native English speaker. Never underestimate the value of this simple capability. The vast majority of clients request Native English speakers only. You would be amazed at how many freelancers from non-English countries submit proposals saying their English is superb. Unfortunately, for these freelancers, most proposals are written in broken English.
- My writing specialties are: fiction and nonfiction writer; blogger; reviewer; and, editor.
- My expertise is specifically stated: medical; education; legal; insurance; and, pet fields.
- My work is not stuffed full of filler words. I am

promising clients informative output.

Then, I add an emotional drawing factor by saying I consider my career as an advocacy opportunity and how important that is to me. They are guaranteed three reputable resources for each article.

- My standards are high and work with avoidable errors will not be submitted.

Be prepared to back up what you have stated in your resume. I say this more than once in *Freelance Writing Express*: your reputation as a writer lies solely on your written words.

Your Guarantee

The next element of your profile is what you promise the client you will deliver. This is my guarantee:

> "My objective is to provide quality writing services tailored to your requirements and satisfaction. A heavy emphasis is placed on determination of the best approach to your project through in-depth interaction and constant communications. A schedule of progress updates can be implemented as requested."

It is short and simple, but to the point. You can add more detail if you desire, but I would keep it from being overly lengthy. Clients are typically in a hurry when they are plowing through proposals. Just provide succinct facts.

Payment Terms

You may be asked to fill out a section regarding payment. I recommend you state:

"Payment terms, turnaround time, and all other details to be confirmed at the time of acceptance of project."

Keywords

There might be a *keywords* area where you can list a specified number of keywords to draw clients searching for freelancers to your profile. Examples are creative fiction writer, fiction writer, nonfiction writer, blogger, reviewer, copywriting, editing, and articles. You know your own expertise best. Choose wide-ranging *keywords* that cover the spectrum of your abilities.

Education, Certificates & Licenses

List every relevant degree, program, and course you have undertaken. By relevant, I mean everything that has to do with your expertise fields. If you claim an expertise in pets and have taken your puppy for successive training programs, list it. I include Continuing Legal Education courses I completed twenty years prior. It complements my claim of expertise.

Work History

Once again, do not worry if you do not have past employment positions strictly related to writing. Your employment history is part of your expertise. It demonstrates you have worked in that particular field, you have hands-on experience and knowledge, and are dependable.

Not all of the freelance websites I recommend in *Freelance Writing Express* require or give you the opportunity to input all of the information contained in this chapter. I chose to cover all of the possible options to provide you with recommendations for whichever components the freelance website profile page permits.

An example of a poorly written overview/profile:

Word Guru is my nickname. How i knit up words to make them expensive to the core is a God given talent which i embrace with much honour, integrity and Determination. Quite Frankly, Perfection is the only thing i tolerate for my clients. I write for Passion, Depth and Insight. I have won several company awards for my great writing skills. I have worked as an editor in China, Australia,Canada and Africa. I take pride in my work. i deliver within deadlines and i am capable of following strict directions as well as conceptualizing solutions that will work for my client..

Glaring errors in this overview/profile include punctuation, capitalization, and incomprehensibility (How i knit up words to make them expensive to the core...?). As a client, I would take one look at this profile and move on.

Leverage your profile with every possible angle. Above all, create a professional, concise profile so, when a prospective client reviews your page, he or she is immediately impressed.

Quick Summary

- Your profile is your irrevocable first impression
- Upload a professional headshot
- Include your skills, past work experience, education, certifications, licences, and hobbies, if relevant
- Ensure your areas of writing expertise, guarantee of credible research resources, superior English, grammar, spelling, and professionalism are noted
- Add *keywords* if this option is available

Remember the receptionist? This is your opportunity to create a superb first impression. It truly makes a difference in whether you receive invitations to projects.

The next chapter is an overview of Constant Content, which is where you start earning the real money.

CHAPTER 13
CONSTANT CONTENT OVERVIEW

"Don't give up the ship."
~ James Lawrence, June 1, 1813

The time has come to put all of your preparation work together to generate income from freelance writing.

Constant Content is a content broker, which means you write an article on whatever topic you wish and list it for sale on Constant Content. Your portfolio catalog includes all approved articles for customers to browse and purchase. Constant Content claims to be one of the largest online content brokers and, with 70,000 writers, it is conceivably a legitimate claim.

I am going to be upfront and honest. Constant Content is strict and demands near perfection from its writers. There are extensive writers' guidelines, some of which we delve into later in this chapter.

I have heard more than one writer say Constant Content is too tough for them and it is not worth it. I beg to differ. If you cannot make it as a writer for Constant Content, you either need to brush up on your writing skills or opt for another career. This may sound harsh, but it is reality. Freelance writing is a highly competitive occupation. Only the best stand out and make a decent income.

Quality is paramount and excellence is guaranteed. Constant Content only accepts writers with the highest levels of grammar and style and a proven ability to create high quality content. — Constant Content

I am confident you can pass Constant Content's editors' expectations by studying the guidelines closely and adhering to its policies. You must either possess the appropriate skills, or be willing and open-minded to educate yourself further.

Author Registration

The first step is to complete the *Author Registration*. You need a pen name (one that sounds professional), along with your legal name, email address, city, state or province, phone number, company name (if you have one), and PayPal account email address for payments.

There is a section for *Education and Expertise*. List all certifications and/or degrees you possess. Tick off all relevant boxes in *Expertise*. In the expertise section, you do not require a certificate or degree to claim expertise. Life experiences, work experience, and hobby knowledge are all you need to qualify for most expertise categories.

Constant Content requires all applicants to take a short quiz prior to acceptance. You are given five questions and asked to identify whether there are punctuation, grammar, or capitalization errors, or no errors in five sentences. You must score four out of five to pass. You have two chances to pass the quiz.

There are a number of different quizzes, but one I obtained has the following five sentences for you to identify punctuation, grammar or spelling errors:

1. Whether or not we go on the picnic depends upon the weather conditions.
2. The quick brown fox jumped over the lazy dog.
3. The color of this sofa is amid a blue and a green.
4. The mailman bring mail every day.
5. All though things in that room are books.

It is not terribly difficult, and you are more than capable of acing the quiz.

Submitting an Article

Once you are past the gatekeepers, create your profile, keeping in mind the information we talked about in Chapter 12. Remember, you want to make your profile appealing to prospective buyers, which means a professional headshot, businesslike SEO-based prose, and include as many skills and/or keywords as possible.

Finally, it is time to submit an article. All articles are reviewed by human editors, rather than through software. This is where the going may get a little rough. Your article may be rejected more than once.

Oftentimes, an editor finds a problem within the first couple paragraphs and sends the article back to the writer for correction. When you receive an article back for revision, correct the issue the editor has indicated and—very important—ensure you go over the entire article again. Sometimes the editors stop at those first paragraphs and assume you carry on throughout the entire article.

Multiple rejections are common. Do not be discouraged or give up. This is a valuable content broker, where you can make good money. I have an example of one of the many Constant Content opportunities at the end of this chapter, so bear with me.

Submission Form

I will take you step-by-step through submission of your article. Constant Content has its particular form by which you must abide precisely. The submission form is located by clicking on the *Submit Article* tab on the left-hand side of the home page under the general tab *My Account*. *My Account* is where you access all information connected with your account.

Insert the title of your article in the first box as shown in the screen shot. Check *Auto-Capitalize* if the box is not already pre-checked. Review the rules for capitalization of titles to make sure you have entered your title correctly.

Every article must fit into a category. In the second box, click on the drop-down menu - *Select Category* – to choose the relevant category.

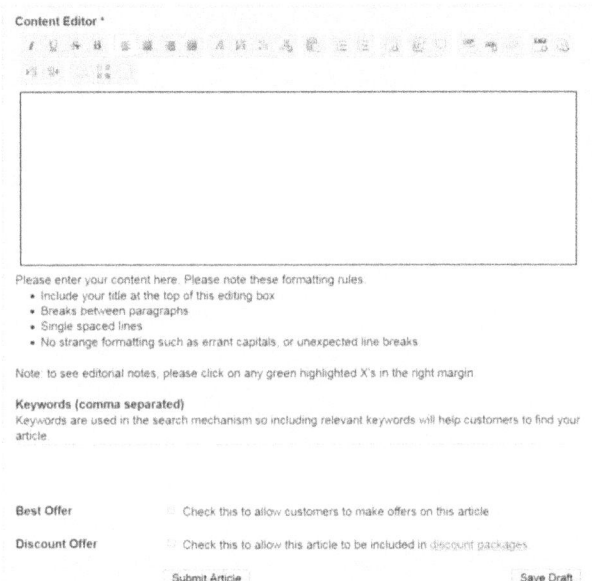

Is This For A Request?

There are five options:

- Not For A Request (this is the option you choose for your first article)
- Public Request
- Writer Pool Request
- Private Request
- Standing Request

These options are discussed in further detail in this chapter.

Setting Prices

Constant Content is different in that you set the price for the article. Have a look at other articles in the same niche to get a feel for pricing. Do not sell yourself short. You want to earn a reasonable amount for the time spent researching and writing the article. At the same time, you do not want to price yourself out of the market.

It may take a bit of time to get pricing down pat. You can edit the cost of the article in your portfolio at any time.

Constant Content works on a commission basis. The company retains 35 percent of the sale price, and you receive the remaining 65 percent. Keep this in mind when setting your prices.

Constant Content has three categories for pricing:

Usage

The client may purchase your article for their own purposes and add links. They may not make changes to the article text and may only use it once. Usage articles can be purchased several times by multiple clients; however, once the article has been sold a number of times, it is no longer attractive to clients as it is already in widespread usage.

Unique

The client has the same rights as usage, with the added opportunities of using the article multiple times rather than just once. Once an article is sold for unique rights, it is removed from the Constant Content system and is no longer available for sale.

Full Rights

The client has all the rights listed in usage and unique, plus they can change the article wording, take credit for the content, and resell the article.

Writers typically charge a tier rate based on usage, unique and full rights. A quick browse of content for sale shows:

- An article about "5 Tips for Rapid Weight Loss" is priced at $20 for usage, $30 for unique rights and

$50 for full rights;

- Another article regarding "Making the Sale: It's All in the Preparation" is marked as $70 for all categories;
- Many writers have opted not to sell their article for unique rights, only for usage and full rights;
- Several writers have listed their article for usage rights only in the hopes they can sell it multiple times and earn more from the article than selling it for unique or full rights.

The screen shot below is Constant Content's pricing guide based on word count. As it states, it is generic and does not take into account the subject matter, which can greatly influence the amount a client is willing to pay for an article.

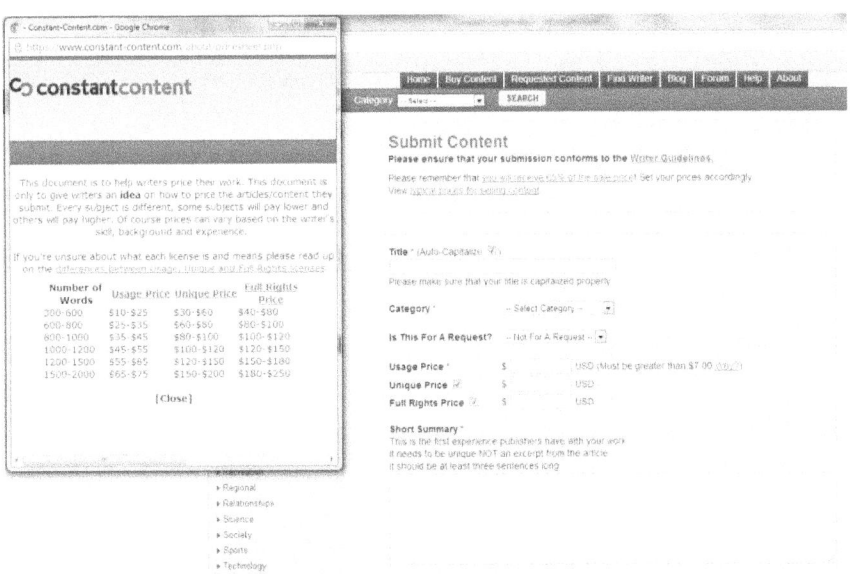

You have the option at the bottom of the submission form of checking *Best Offer* to permit customers to make offers on the articles or *Discount Offer* to permit the articles to be included in discount packages. My review of content listed for sale revealed many writers permitted a *Best Offer*, while none included their article in discount packages.

If your article has been for sale for a long period of time, you can either adjust your prices or, perhaps, check *Best Offer*. I do not recommend you include it in a discount package.

It is important to keep in mind the article might receive a lot of hits before it sells. Do not be discouraged if there is a high number of hits but no sale. One of my articles had 99 hits before it sold.

Try not to focus on the number of hits an article receives but, rather, keep writing and submitting content. You must have written for Constant Content within the previous 60 days to appear in search results.

Patience is key. It is pointless to torment yourself checking every few hours or, even, every day how many hits your articles receive. When it sells, you receive an email from Constant Content advising of the sale.

Ninety-eight percent of my articles sold for full rights. The other two percent were for usage.

Short Summary

The short summary is meant solely for your sales pitch. Do not include any portion of your article or identical wording in this box. It must be at least three sentences long. This is your opportunity to make your best pitch. You want to give thought to the short summary to make it attractive to potential customers.

Long Summary

The long summary is the entire article you post in *Content Editor* in the next step. Unless you change your default settings, 100 percent of the article will be visible. I recommend you reset the default percentage to forty percent.

Click on the link *account settings* to change the default. You are redirected to your *My Account Details* tab.

Showing 100 percent of your article might be a tad dangerous. Although a prospect cannot copy and paste your article, they could take the time to retype it if they have two monitors.

Content Editor

This is where you paste your article. I say "paste" for a reason. The content editor has the functionality for you to type and format your article directly in the box. I dissuade you from doing this for a number of reasons.

Firstly, the box is too small and you can only see portions of your article at a time. Secondly, this prevents a thorough REP as we discussed in Chapter 10. Thirdly, it is crucial you have a copy of all articles you have written stored on your computer to use as samples for your portfolio. After all, this is how you are building your portfolio (and making money at the same time).

You can edit your article in the content box if you realize you missed formatting, such as underlining or bold. There are a limited number of formatting codes in the content box.

This screen shot shows the available codes. No codes other than those listed below are allowed.

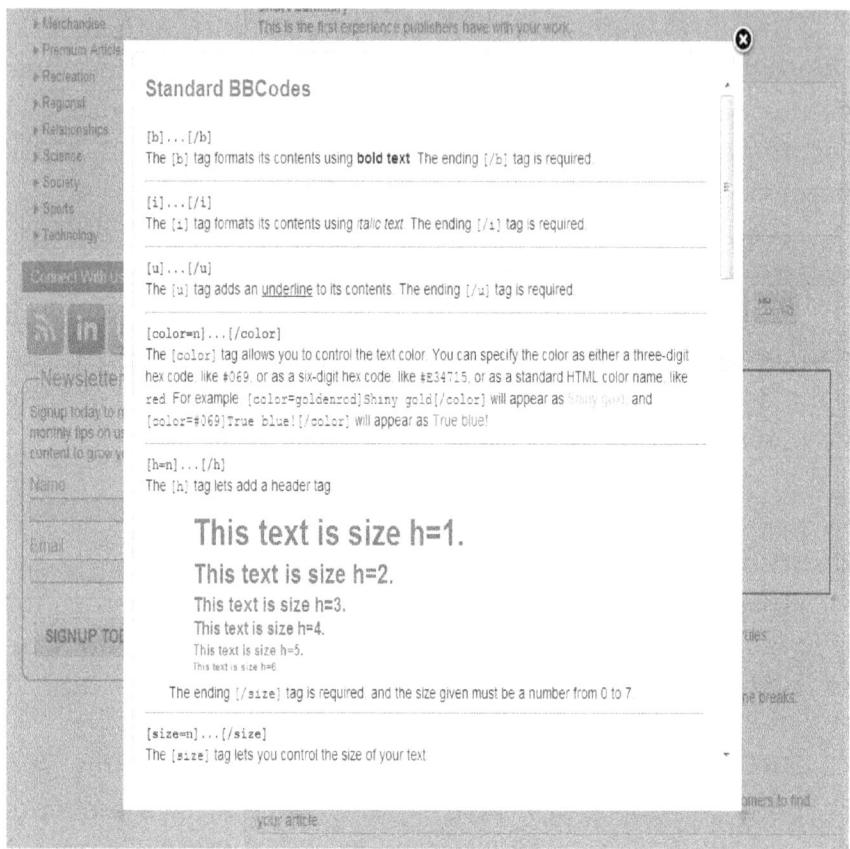

Submit your article in single-spaced Times New Roman or Arial 12 pt. Use double spaces between paragraphs.

Keywords

The final box on the submission form is for inclusion of keywords customers might use to search for content such as the article you are submitting. Include as many relevant keywords as possible. Separate the keywords with commas.

We talked about keywords in Chapter 7. It may be helpful to go back and use the information in that chapter to determine appropriate keywords.

Submit Article

This is the biggest—and scariest—moment you may encounter in commencing your freelance writing career: clicking the *Submit Article* button. I was nervous the first time I submitted an article, and I have talked to countless writers who all felt the same.

It is normal. Few writers are fearless of their first submission. It gets easier each time. Your confidence naturally grows and, before you know, hitting the *Submit Article* does not faze you one bit.

Expect it might take up to five days for review of your article. Constant Content claims it attempts to complete reviews within two to three days, but there is no guarantee this will happen.

Once the article is approved, Constant Content lists it on your catalog and customers can preview the first one-third of the article. This is automatically defaulted by Constant Content. You do not have to do anything. Constant Content watermarks articles to prevent appropriation by unscrupulous buyers or hackers.

Home

Now we will examine the various tabs listed on the left-hand side of the *Home* tab in order of listing, with the exception of one tab: *Submit Article*. I placed this tab at the beginning of this chapter for logistical reasons. If you have not submitted an article first, many tabs are difficult to understand.

Account Status Tab

The *Account Status* tab is your financial information. It shows the payment due to you by Constant Content for the current month. Constant Content pays out into your PayPal account on the first business day of each month.

Here you find the number of your articles under review and received offers under review.

If you have a blog, you can insert a Constant Content widget to promote your articles. The HTML is available on this page.

On the top left-hand side of the page, the newest requests are listed. Recent document sales (of other writers) are below in a chart denoting title, category, and license type. Search topics are listed in a chart showing recent and popular subjects.

My Profile

My Profile lists basic information, such as your availability, how many articles you have sold, tabs for clients to request content or contact you, your brief bio, location, education, certification, and areas of expertise.

Inbox Tab

Here you find messages received, notifications about articles reviewed, accepted, and sold, payments made by Constant Content, and messages you have sent.

Notifications Tab

The *Notification Tab* has three categories: Messages; Notifications; Sent Messages. Click on the appropriate category to access information.

My Projects Tab

The content under the *My Projects* is entitled *Writer Dashboard.*

This is an interactive calendar where you can track projects you have been invited to and due dates, and what requests are available.

You can add notes to supplement project details. A separate calendar is used for each individual project, which is accessed by the dropdown menu at the top right.

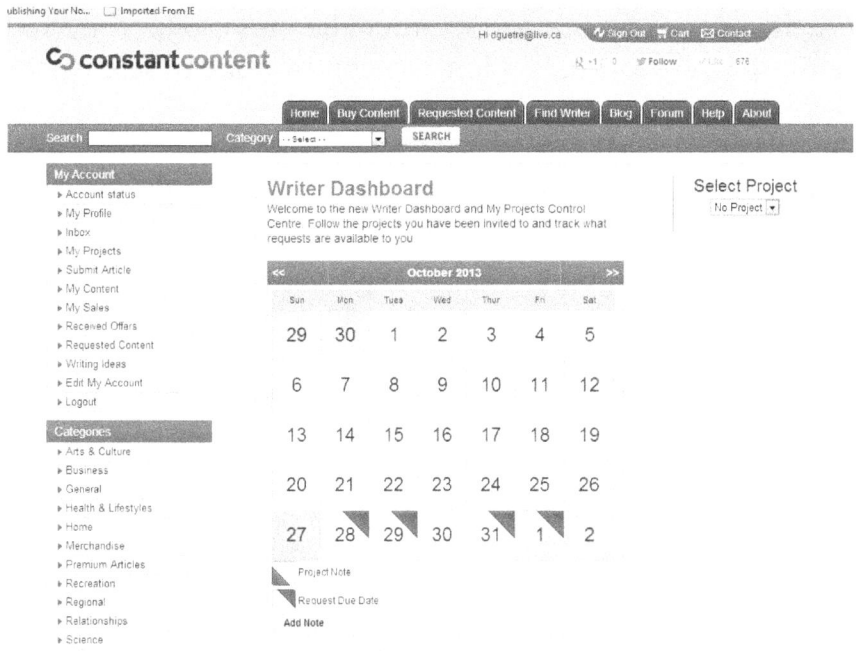

Underneath the calendar is a graph of available requests and access to messages in your *Inbox.*

Clients may add you to their "team" for a *Project*, which basically means they work with select writers. If you are a member of a team, you can claim requests to work on the client's *Project* from this tab.

My Revisions Requests

If your article is returned for revisions—it is a possibility—the editor's notes are provided with inline comments. You can work off those notes directly in the content editor. You can save a draft of the article if you do not have the time to fully complete the revisions in one sitting.

When you revise an article as per an editor's comments, make sure you copy and replace the article on your computer.

Should a prospective client desire to purchase an

article from your catalog but would like revisions, they can request you make specific revisions to your article either before or after they purchase it. This is available only for *Full Rights* articles. You can accept or reject the request. Should you accept the revision request, you can complete it for free or negotiate with the client for an extra charge. If you are willing to offer a limited number of free revisions on your catalog content, note this in your bio.

Content written for requests is handled differently. Clients are allowed two free revisions after they purchase your article, with any further revision charges to be negotiated between you and the client.

Negotiations can include counterproposals by either party in both of the above situations. The exception to this guideline is you cannot counter propose for the first two free revisions included in request content.

You must wait until the client has responded to your rejection or counterproposal to proceed with revisions.

Constant Content sends you a notification for *Revisions Requests*. Under the *My Revisions Requests* tab on your account, the title of the article appears. Click on the link to see the requested revisions.

If it is part of the two free revisions or you and the client have agreed on payment for revisions, click the *Begin Revisions* button. A content editor screen appears where you read the changes requested and make revisions.

When you are finished, click the *Save Work* button to save the revised article. Then click the *Submit Revision* button. This notifies the client that the revisions are complete.

The client then has three options:
- Accept the revised article
- Request further revisions
- Reject the article (in the case of catalog content)

The screenshot below shows the tabs under the *My Revisions Requests* where you track information:

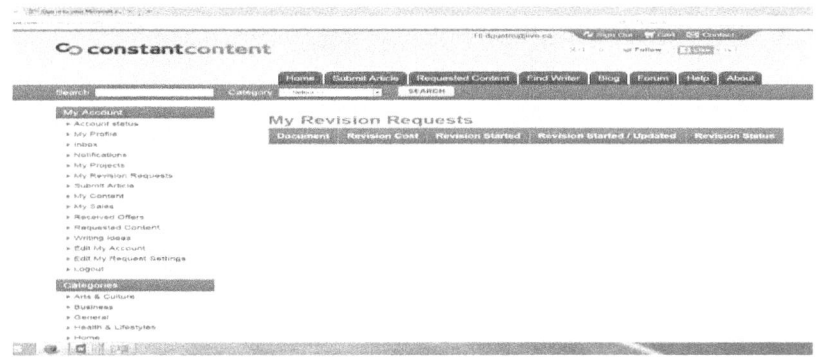

My Content Tab

My Content is exactly just that—all your content whether it be sold, viewed, reviewed, unfinished, rejected, or resubmitted. The dropdown menu lists these options.

My Sales Tab

The best tab of all—your sold content.

Received Offers Tab

If you ticked *Best Offer* when submitting articles, this is the tab where any such offers made are found. You can accept offers; however, the customers must complete payment before the transaction is considered complete. The articles are not removed from your catalog until paid for, and other customers still have the option of purchasing them.

Requested Content Tab

Requested Content is set out in a graph determined by filters. The filters are automatically defaulted to All Requests.

I will break down the various types of *Requested*

Content:

Public Requests
These are open invitations to all writers:

Call for Articles
The client submits an open invitation for all writers to submit articles. The article length, price, and closing date are included in the graph.

Standing Requests
Standing Requests are posted when Constant Content identifies topics that are selling well. Submitting articles to a *Standing Request* does not keep those articles in reserve for a particular client. The public can still purchase them. So, in fact, you are submitting for consideration via two different avenues. This is a good thing.

Casting Calls
The client expresses an interest in hiring a writer to work on projects. The client details the specifics and expected qualifications. You email the client directly to discuss the project and further communications.

Writer Pool Requests
These request are available only to writers who have a minimum of ten articles accepted by Constant Content's editors. Once this has occurred, you are assigned an *Access Level*. The lower your *Access Level*, the sooner you can claim the request. For instance, *Access Level* 1 has first dibs. If an *Access Level* 1 writer does not claim the request within a specified time, *Access Level* 2 writers then qualify to claim the request, and so on up the *Access Level* ladder.

Your *Access Level* is also dependent on whether your

profile is complete and the percentage of articles submitted that are accepted without revision requests.

A client requesting the below categories can target writers based on location, certification, expertise, content topics, and other information. The idea is that Constant Content matches clients with qualified writers.

Targeted Requests

These requests are visible if the client's project description targets your skills and experience. You may claim these requests and commence work. It is best to claim the requests immediately so the client is aware you are on the job.

Expert Groups

You must apply and be accepted into *Expert Groups* to claim requests. There are several categories in *Expert Groups*. You must complete a written application for each group individually, and Constant Content editors will advise you of their decision. Applications are made through your *Edit My Request Settings* tab (more information to follow).

My Requests

These requests are received from clients who wish to work solely with you. They are invisible to other Constant Content writers.

Private Requests

These are requests from clients who specify they have selected you to work on their projects. *Private Requests* are made when the client applies for writing services and delivered directly to you.

Claimed Requests

You must claim all *Private Requests*.

Completed Requests

The title says it all. These are your completed *Private Requests*.

Acquiring a client through *Private Requests* has the benefits of a predetermined rate, number of articles desired, and assurance the client purchases the articles. Select *Private Requests* when submitting the articles.

Message the client with any queries and, also, keep them updated on your progress on their project. A happy customer is repeat business and referrals.

Writing Ideas Tab

Lost for words? The *Writing Ideas* page lists Category Sales (with recently sold content delineated), Categories (broken down from broad generalization into specific topics with the number of articles for sale on each precise topic), and Search Topics (with recent search topics and most popular search topics in the last three months).

While this can be helpful, I strongly advise you write in the expertise areas you identified earlier. Writing for requests, if they fall within your niche, can be profitable.

Following trends about which you have little knowledge will not serve you well. You will spend an inordinate amount of time on research, and there is no guarantee the article will be picked up by the customer who made the request. Over 80 percent of sales are made from the Constant Content catalog. Your odds of making sales through prolifically writing content for your catalog are greater than chasing trends.

Edit My Account

This tab permits you to change your personal information. It also provides you with a summary of your total amount earned and frequency of payment.

Remember the long summary when submitting an article? You reset the long summary percentage default here at any time.

Email preferences for notices and password changes can be selected under this tab.

Edit My Request Settings

This tab is where you:

- set your status—available or idle
- apply to Expert Groups
- locate your Access Level
- list your Education and Expertise
- select your Areas of Expertise
- indicate your preferable Content Types (i.e. articles; copywriting; web contents; blogs)
- specify if you are fluent in a foreign language.

The *Edit My Request Settings* is your most important tab if you wish to work on *Requests*. It must be kept up-to-date to ensure you have every opportunity to receive *Requests*.

Blog, Forums, and Help

Tabs for these topics are found at the top of the Constant Content website. The *Forums* can be informative as long as you separate the wheat from the chaff. There is a fair amount of writer whining in *Forums*, but there are tidbits worth considering and implementing. Use your excellent judgment to discern what to take to heart.

Read the FAQ, which should answer just about any question.

Writers' Guidelines

There is an extended form of guidelines available on Constant Content's website (https://www.constant-content.com/about/extended_guidelines.htm). I will not go through them in detail. Rather, I shall pick out what I know is important, and I leave it to you to read the remainder. General pointers are included here to highlight common practices or errors. They are not exhaustive. Once again, I urge you to read the guidelines yourself. I stress this recommendation because Constant Content is extremely exacting in their expectations.

Readability Principles

Your writing must be cohesive and coherent to present a focused and organized article. *Readability* is a priority. Remain on track with your subject and do not include irrelevant information. Remember, you can use a Flesch-Kincaid online tool or the Word function as mentioned in Chapter 10.

Introductory Paragraph

The introductory paragraph sets the stage for your article. Readers understand what type of information is to be presented in your article from information in the introductory paragraph.

You must always write with the reader in mind. Your audience is first and foremost. Failure to keep the reader at the forefront loses your audience, and also ensures your article is rejected for revisions. If you are uncertain about how to write an introductory paragraph, there are resources you can Google to learn about the principles of introductory paragraphs.

Wording

Constant Content is rigorous in cutting excess verbiage

in articles. Write lean, cutting out unnecessary words or phrases. Never begin your sentences with "There are", "There is", etc. These words can usually be eliminated by rewording your sentences.

Avoid awkward wording. If it does not sound natural when you read it aloud, it probably is awkwardly written. Play around with your sentence structure for a logical flow of words.

Pronouns and antecedents must agree. If you are unsure about this concept, read http://www.towson.edu/ows/pro_antagree.htm for the nine rules of pronoun-antecedents agreement.

Use comparative adjectives only when comparing objects, philosophies, etc. Writing "LED bulbs are brighter." is unacceptable. Acceptable is, "LED bulbs are brighter than incandescent bulbs."

Grammar

A few items to note:
- Ensure verb consistency
- "Would" and "could" are heavily discouraged
- The Oxford (serial) comma is acceptable as long as there is consistency
- US or UK English is permitted
- Vary sentence structure
- Absolutely no run-on sentences
- No dangling modifiers
- Write parallel constructive sentences

Miscellaneous

Other noteworthy guidelines include:
- No editorial or opinion articles
- No creative writing
- No first-person point-of-view
- Second-person point-of-view is acceptable
- The pronoun "one" is not acceptable

- Content must be of value to the reader
- Lists are acceptable within an article, but an article cannot consist of merely a list
- Articles cannot make reference to other articles
- No article series permitted
- Prejudicial and/or stereotypical content is unacceptable
- Brand names must be spelled correctly with appropriate capitalization
- No hyperlinks are permitted in the article content, but website references without the URL are allowed
- No bylines or biographical information permitted

We have reached the end of a long overview chapter on Constant Content. It is a lot of information to digest at once. My advice is to read through this chapter a few times before you submit your first article. Each reading assists you to locate relevant information you need at that precise moment.

As a bit of inspiration, I recently received a message from Constant Content that an article I had written six years earlier had sold again. Constant Content can be an excellent source of passive income.

Constant Content will transform you into an awesome writer, capable of surmounting all challenges in your career. There is no doubt in my mind you can and will be a successful Constant Content freelance writer with the application of the methods and strategies discussed in this chapter and earlier ones.

Quick Summary
- Constant Content is a broker where you list content for sale
- You set prices for *usage*, *unique*, and *full rights*
- Constant Content has rigorous standards

- Read and strictly follow the writers' guidelines
- Articles must be submitted in accordance with the submission form
- Your article may be rejected more than once
- Prospective clients can request revisions, which are accommodated through the revision system
- You are permitted to negotiate revision charges with clients
- Additional writing opportunities are *Call for Articles, Casting Calls, Targeted Requests, Expert Group* opportunities, and *private requests*
- Ensure your *Edit My Request Settings* tab is current
- Persevere. Constant Content can be extremely profitable

Only have a few hours to spare? The next chapter will profitably fill those hours.

CHAPTER 14
CROWDSOURCE

"Life is a series of steps. Things are done gradually. Once in a while there is a giant step, but most of the time we are taking small, seemingly insignificant steps on the stairway of life."
~ Ralph Ransom, Artist (d. 1908)

CrowdSource **can be** a gem for additional income. If you need to fill in gaps between other income sources, an unexpected expense crops up, or you want to save to treat yourself, CrowdSource is an ideal solution.

This is not a bid website or a content broker. Assignments are available for all writers—you need only click on the *Write Article* button to claim the assignment.

CrowdSource is a platform that offers *microtasks*. To gain access to assignments, you must first pass a writing assessment. You have approximately six subjects predetermined by CrowdSource from which to choose. It must be a minimum of 300 words and contain the SEO keywords noted in the article choice.

Carefully read the instructions before you write the assessment and print off the sample writing assignment. CrowdSource writing is a tad different from other freelance sites.

CrowdSource uses the Associated Press Stylebook (AP

Style).

For the writing assessment, you must follow their format exactly. Begin with an introduction to the topic, followed by three subsections—the titles of which must be in question format—, and end with your conclusion.

I chose to write about leukemia treatment. I am now repurposing that writing assessment to list on Constant Content for sale. Never waste a word that can earn you income.

It takes two to three business days before CrowdSource accepts or rejects your submission. This is simple and easy work. There is no reason for rejection, unless you forget REP. I copied my assessment from the CrowdSource form into Word to ensure I did not make silly goofs.

When you are accepted—because you will be—CrowdSource sends an email with a *WorkStation Invitation*. You login through your PayPal account to activate the link sent by CrowdSource.

A third email from CrowdSource advises you of your *WorkStation Qualification*. You are designated an *Answer Writer* at level determined by the quality of your writing sample. The three emails are sent almost simultaneously.

Once you log in—through your PayPal or Facebook accounts—click on your name to access your profile. Your profile does not require you to fill in information.

You will see the acronym "HIT" in several areas on CrowdSource. This stands for "Human Intelligence Task".

Profile
Your profile lists:

Summary Data Payment — Owed $X for Y tasks approved; Pending $X for Z tasks awaiting approval

Summary Activity Data — Earnings $X; Approvals Y/Z; Approval Rate % (with Gold Rated for approvals of 99% to 100%)

Qualifications — Tells you how many qualifications you have, with the number of active tasks. A bar lists:
- Name (Answer Writer)
- Available Tasks (1,000+)
- Last Worked
- Approved (x)
- Pass Rate (%)
- Earned ($X)

Subscriptions — you check or uncheck boxes for email notifications for various categories. Within the *Subscriptions* section there is a list of different tasks available. Beside each task category, a date shows when you last worked on that particular category

Recent Work Summary — This section shows when your last submission was received and how many tasks you submitted in the last seven days.

You can set your work hours, days per week, hourly and weekly target rates, work preferences, and experience or interests at the bottom of this page.

CrowdSource Workforce Support

CrowdSource is thorough with their guidelines and training materials. These are accessed by clicking the *?* next to your profile name. There are four categories under *Workforce Support: Home; Solutions; Tickets*; and, *Forums*.

A section under the *Home* category entitled *General* walks you through the process of writing for CrowdSource. Samples abound for every type of assignment, along with webinars, tips, and style guides.

Forums is where you find the latest announcements from CrowdSource, along with discussions between writers and CrowdSource staff.

Find Work

The *Find Work* button is at the top of the screen. Click on *Find Work* and a screen similar to the one below appears.

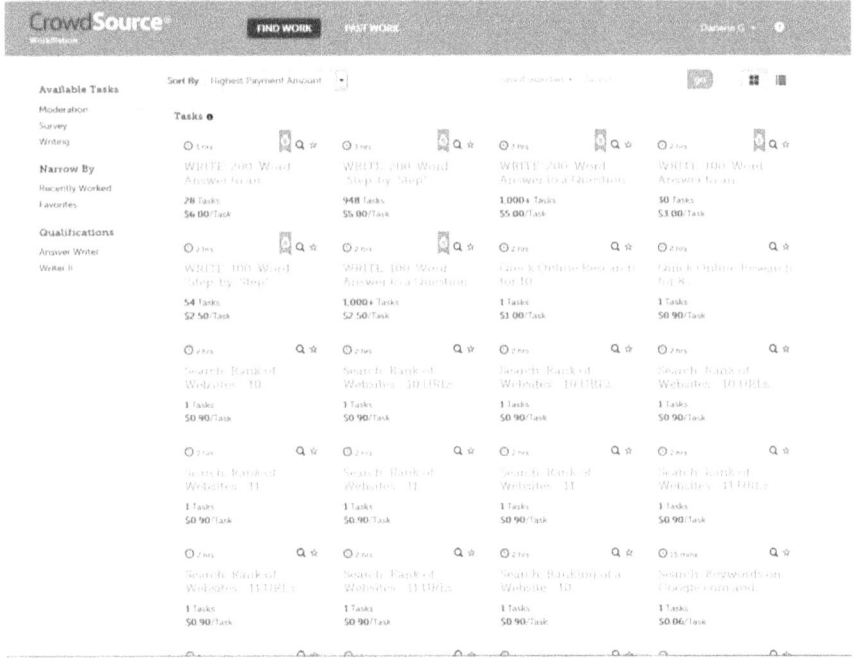

Here you find tasks of various natures and compensation. There are icons at the top of each job description:

- *Clock* — The time limit in which to complete the task is located to the right of the clock.
- *Magnifying Glass* — Permits you to preview the task

and provides clear instructions on how to complete it, with supporting links to examples and further guidelines.

- *Star* — Allows you to mark a task as a *favorite.*
- *Green Ribbon with Dollar Sign* — CrowdSource has a weekly bonus plan. The *green ribbon with a dollar sign* indicates the assignment is eligible for the bonus plan.

The bonus plan applies only to 100 and 200 word answers and 100 and 200 "step-by-step" answers.

There are tiers, with graduated bonuses earned for number of assignments completed. For example:

- Tier 1 may be 3 assignments for a bonus of $4
- Tier 2 may be 5 assignments for a bonus of $8
- Tier 3 may be 8 assignments for a bonus of $16
- Tier 4 may be 12 assignments for a bonus of $28
- Tier 5 may be 16 assignments for a bonus of $42
- Tier 6 may be 20 assignments for a bonus of $57
- Tier 7 may be 28 assignments for a bonus of $81

The above figures are examples only. They are not set in stone. Weekly tiers and bonus amounts vary according to CrowdSource's production goals. CrowdSource sends emails outlining the tiers and bonuses, typically at the beginning of each month.

The screenshot below illustrates how assignments are tracked for bonuses.

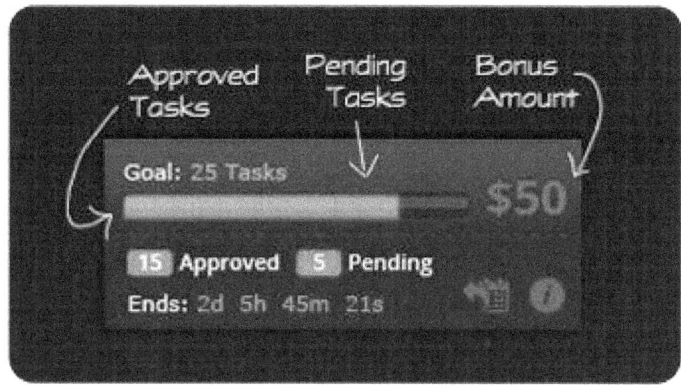

Microtask assignments include:

Google Searches:

These are simple *microtasks* that pay incremental amounts in cents, but they can often be completed within one minute. You are limited to the number of search tasks you are permitted to complete.

An example is locating URLs for four different keywords. I did this as a test assignment as part of my research for this chapter. I was finished within the minute. It only paid $0.08, but the point is it was fast and easy.

Two days later, CrowdSource deposited $0.08 into my PayPal account.

Write a 100 or 200 word answer to a Question:

The instructions are specific and include resource rules with lists of approved and unapproved sites, how to write the answer, technical guidelines, style guidelines, answer types, and question guidelines.

CrowdSource requires its content written in an Inverted Pyramid Format:

Answer Section:

Should directly answer the question with the most important information in the first two to four sentences;

Additional Information Section:
Give important details that are crucial to the overall answer in the next two to four sentences;

Additional Information Section:
In the last one to two sentences include relevant, interesting details.
Resource links must be included with the answer.

Write a 100 or 200 word "Step-by-Step" Answer:
Instructions are once again explicit. You must include accepted resource links.

Introduction Section:
Introduce the process you are going to detail in 20 to 40 words, including any preparation or information required beforehand, the estimated time it takes to complete the process, and note materials required for completion of the process.

Steps Sections:
Outline and explain each step. Create headings for each step that begin with an action verb that explains the step briefly. Do not use punctuation at the end of the heading.

Steps are to be written sequentially and include all necessary actions to complete the process. The objective is to write a *Step-by-Step* answer readers can follow without difficulty.

Why CrowdSource?

There are several crowdsourcing sites, but CrowdSource offers the best remuneration and has thousands of assignments.

The surest method of making the most of CrowdSource is to write 200 answers with bonuses, as they offer the best pay. It might be slow to begin with while you become familiar with their guidelines but, once you have the hang of it, you can easily write four answers in an hour. You receive the base rate, plus applicable bonuses dependent on the number of answers you write per week.

I advise you write one of each type of question and await approval first, rather than pounding out a bunch of answers. I say this because you do not want your approval rating to suffer.

CrowdSource Writing Levels

Advancement to a higher writing level and better pay is dependent on the quality of your work and your approval rate. Once you have advanced to a higher writing level, you must maintain an applicable approval rate or you are demoted to a lower level. The maintenance approval rate is typically five to seven percent less than the approval rate required to advance.

Level 1 has the lowest approval rate (currently in the 60th percentile), with Level V at the highest (currently in the 90th percentile). Keep in mind these approval rates are subject to fluctuation.

Your level rating is influenced by the number of small infractions or a major infraction. A one-time minor infraction does not affect your writing level. You must know the guidelines inside and out for success on CrowdSource. Make sure you spend the appropriate amount of time learning the rules and regulations before you jump in.

You do not need to write a minimum number of writing tasks to advance, but you do have to complete an assigned amount of tasks to advance to a higher writing level. A *Progress Bar*—which is located in the *Tool Taskbar*—indicates the number of tasks required to move up to the next level.

CrowdSource will not meet your monthly income goals but, because of the brevity and simplicity of assignments, it can become monthly supplemental income between projects or while waiting for Constant Content articles to sell.

The vital message I discern from my research is CrowdSource insists on quality writing and strict adherence to guidelines.

Quick Summary
- CrowdSource is a *microtask* platform
- A writing assessment is required prior to acceptance
- CrowdSource adheres to the Associated Press Stylebook
- Writers are assigned varying levels
- Each *microtask* pays a specified amount and must be completed within the specified time
- Some *microtasks* qualify for bonuses
- Your rating level is dependent on the quality of your work and approval rate
- CrowdSource is a source of supplemental income

Ready for the last freelance writing market segment? The next chapter focuses on freelance bid websites.

CHAPTER 15
HOW FREELANCE BID WEBSITES OPERATE

"The essence of strategy is choosing what not to do."
~ Michael E. Porter, Professor and Director
Institute for Strategy and Competitiveness, Harvard
Business School

The Internet is littered with freelance bid websites, which are commonly called "content mills".   The naysayers and haters of content mills are correct in the majority of cases. Writers are paid pennies per hour, competition is fierce, and, typically, the lowest bid wins.   I have researched freelance bid websites, searched high and low for years, and reached the conclusion that the income sources contained in *Freelance Writing Express* offer the best opportunities.

Recently, a student I mentored contacted me about a freelance writing website. It sounded fabulous. All you paid was a one-time $34 fee, and you had access to thousands of the best businesses with assignments a seventh-grader could write. She asked what I thought. It took me five minutes to discover this website had over 300 complaints registered with the Better Business Bureau in the two previous years. Few were resolved. I then read different blogs reviewing this website. Not one was positive nor was it recommended.

If you do choose to explore other websites, please practice your due diligence. Research the website before you plunk down your money. The website I mention above is a grab and run operation. Do not be fooled by the "Guaranteed or Your Money Back!" They take your $34, and then leave you with no recourse to recoup your money, because there is no way to contact them.

That leaves us with the minority of viable income sources. I introduced you to a profitable income source in Chapter 13, Constant Content Overview and a supplemental income source in Chapter 14, CrowdSource. I introduce you to the remaining recommended income sources in later chapters but, first, we need to cover how freelance bid websites operate. This chapter explains the basics of how to navigate freelance bid websites to your benefit.

Basic Premise

Clients post projects on freelance bid websites, and then review bids from contractors (that is you) to make a decision on whom to award the project. Sounds simple, right? It is, and it is not. If you know how to target projects and clients, it is. If you do not know how to navigate projects and select the best clients, it is not simple.

I think it is safe to say the vast majority of new contractors believe they should bid on every project posted, and then cross their fingers they are awarded the much-vaunted first project. Months later, many are still without a project. It is all in the approach, and that is what you are going to learn in this chapter.

How to Locate Projects

First of all, locate a tab called *Find Work* or similar language at the top or on the side of the website. Click on this option to access all projects listed on the site.

Freelance bid websites offer multiple freelance disciplines; however, the category you focus on is *Writing & Translation*. Click on this category and several subcategories, which may include the following, appears:

Article Writing	Editing & Proofreading
Web Content	Academic Writing
Translations	Technical Writing
E-books and Blogs	Sales Writing
Other - Writing Services	Resumes & CoverLetters
Copywriting	Others - Translations
Ghost Writing	Press Releases
Creative Writing	User Guides & Manuals

Next you choose any number of categories you feel are appropriate for your expertise and skill set. Click on the box beside each subcategory and a check mark appears. This narrows the available projects down to the type of projects you seek.

Fixed Price Projects

Further streamline your search by clicking *Fixed Price*. This is one of the most vital components of bidding strategies on freelance bid sites.

Think of *fixed price* projects as working for "flat rate". Flat rate is common in automotive repair shops. The premise is you are paid a fixed amount for a project. If you complete that project in a certain amount of hours that pays you an hourly rate you deserve, then you have broken even.

Now, suppose you finish that project faster than you anticipated. You are now open to accepting another *fixed rate* project. In essence, you are making more than the hourly rate you calculated on the first project, because you completed it in less time and are now working on a second project.

So, back to our automotive mechanic. He is paid $200 to do a tune up on a vehicle and given six hours to do the job. This amounts to $33 an hour. Our automotive mechanic is a talented guy who does top-notch work and does it quickly. He has honed his skills, gets right to business, and keeps his head down working. He finishes the job in four hours. For that job alone, he has made $50 an hour. Now his manager hands him another *fixed price* job. It pays $100 and the time quoted to complete the job is three hours. Our guy finishes in two hours. Another $50 an hour in his pocket.

Look at the time—six hours—he is paid to complete the first job, and then calculate how long it actually took him to complete the first and second job. What do you discover? He has earned $300 in those six hours rather than $200. If he used all of the time he was allotted for both jobs, it would take him eight hours to earn the same money.

This is the goal you want to achieve. There is an important component included in this analogy. One we have talked about in previous chapters. The mechanic worked fast and produced high-quality work at the same time. This is what you must strive for in your work. We cannot sacrifice caliber for expediency, however tempting. That road leads to clientele loss and poor reviews.

Big Brother is Watching

Another reason I discourage hourly rate projects is clients have the option of taking screenshots of you when you have clocked in. This "Big Brother" concept goes against the grain of professionalism. You are a professional freelance writer. You do not require supervision, nor is the invasion of your privacy warranted.

How long would you endure your employer popping in your office several times a day to check if you really are working in an office environment? I know, for me, not long. Either I am a trusted employee and respected as such, or I move on.

Freelance writers often juggle several projects at once. You might be conducting research on one project, while you are proofreading another project. Breaking up tasks, rather than focussing on one project for hours on end, helps prevent mental exhaustion. The final nail in the coffin is most clients offer a ridiculous hourly wage of between $3 and $10 an hour. This is nowhere close to a living wage.

Now, it is time to bid on *fixed price* projects and earn money.

The Early Bird Gets the Project

Make a habit of frequently checking for new projects. I recommend browsing new projects first thing in the morning and later in the afternoon. Try not to fall into the trap of checking every hour. You waste time and interrupt the flow of your work if you are dashing in and out of income sources more than twice a day.

That said, submitting your proposal on new projects within a short time of the project post gives you a hand up in winning the project. Some clients hire within a few hours; some wait days; others never award the project. You want to ensure your proposal is in place for those clients who hire within hours.

As an example of how fast proposals stack up, I looked at a project that had been posted four hours prior. There were already 22 proposals; that number doubled to 44 proposals nine hours after the posting.

Vetting Clients

I mentioned clients who do not award projects. To avoid wasting your bids (which cost you money), there are simple methods to vet these types of clients. I address this crucial element for applicable income sources in Chapters 17 and 20.

Location, Location, Location

Yes, I know it is cliché, but it is relevant. I strongly advise you bid only on projects based in the United States, Canada, United Kingdom, Australia, New Zealand, Israel, and Western Europe. The reason? The pay. Developing countries are used to cheap labor and that is all they want. They request the world, and pay you dirt. This is not discrimination; it is reality.

The Competition

Another strategy to increasing your odds of winning a project is to check out your competition. I do not necessarily do this for every project, but if I think I have a good shot at it, I often do.

Proposals by other freelancers are sealed 99 percent of the time. What this means is you cannot see what they are offering as their fees, and nor can they see what you have indicated as a fee.

You can access other freelancers' profiles by clicking on their name. If they have worked for next to nothing for clients in the past, chances are they are placing a low bid.

Should the project be stacked with freelancers who have worked multiple projects and have low annual earnings, this is a red flag. Divide the number of projects by the amount earned. Another red flag is if the list of freelancers are mostly located in developing countries. Ten dollars a day is a lot of money for these freelancers;

however, it is not a living wage for developed countries.

The competition's earnings and locations may be helpful, but their profile is the best indicator. What is their ranking (to be covered in Chapters 17 and 20)? How does their bio read? Are their work samples well-written? What is their feedback status?

Answers to the above questions either tell you that you stand a good chance or that you are outranked. There is nothing wrong with being outranked. Everyone has to start somewhere. There have been projects I have decided to bypass because other freelancers had more experience, a higher ranking, or, perhaps, were composed of a team.

Bidding against a team is probably not the best idea. There is absolutely no way an individual can write and deliver a project in the same amount of time as five other people working as a whole. If you really feel you are the perfect candidate, have a look at the team's work portfolio. I have seen some shoddy teamwork, which was obviously burped out, and decided to place a proposal.

How Many Projects Should You Bid On?

Good question. In the beginning, bid on as many as you think you are a good fit for. Remember, always, target projects that fall within your expertise and skills. Be choosey. Do not waste your bids on projects you in all likelihood do not stand a chance of winning.

Freelance writing is like any other self-employment business. You never know when you are going to win a proposal or when a client is going to award the project.

Do not be scared to bid on several projects. You might win one, three, or none. If it is none, do not give up. Persevere. It will happen. I promise. I hear of numerous writers who give up because, after bidding for a month or two, they had not received a project.

If you are having no luck with bids, spend time writing

for Constant Content and putting those articles up for sale. Squeeze in a few hours on CrowdSource. There is no such thing as too many proposals in the beginning.

If, by happy chance, you should win—say, four projects—in a short period of time, you have the option of advising the client on every one of the four projects when you can deliver. If you placed a proposal on, for instance, May 13 and said you could deliver within ten days, those ten days do not start until the client awards you the project, *terms and conditions* are finalized, and the client pays your fees into *escrow* (more to come on *escrow*). Therefore, if the client did not award you the project until May 25, you have until June 4 to write and deliver that project.

Now, back to the scheduling. Many pages ago I said the most common mistake new freelancers make is taking on too much work. This is a friendly reminder. Keep it realistic. Only accept as much work as you can handle within the prescribed hours per week you have allotted to freelancing. No work/life balance equals burnout. It is permissible to send "Dear John" letters as I mentioned earlier.

Once your schedule is full, do not bid on any projects. Approximately one week prior to your final project's delivery date, throw out multiple proposals again. Once your schedule is full, stop. Repeat this strategy until retirement.

Sponsored Proposals

Sponsoring your proposal puts you at the top of the list of contractors submitting for that particular project. There are limited spaces for sponsored proposals. I am somewhat hesitant to encourage you to sponsor your proposal unless you are a perfect fit for the project.

Freelance bid websites say sponsored proposals are

advantageous. This, of course, is to their benefit as you are spending bids at a faster rate and, hopefully, purchasing more to replenish your rapidly diminishing bids remaining on your monthly subscription. Another route taken by freelance bid websites is you pay a fee that is charged to your account to move your proposal higher up the list. I have not experienced or seen evidence that sponsored proposals win more projects. A client who is about to spend hundreds of dollars typically reviews more than the three top sponsored proposals.

Rank, average job rating (on a 1 to 5 star system), and positive client reviews are the most valuable commodities you can possess. My belief is these assets trump sponsored proposals.

Terms

When you are awarded a project, there are always *terms and conditions* between you and the client. I discuss how to set up *terms and conditions* in Chapters 17 and 20.

I cannot emphasize enough how important it is to scrutinize and double-check *terms and conditions* when accepting a project. I slipped up a few months ago and it cost me $80. I do not like losing money on a project.

Project Deadlines

Project deadlines are typically 12 AM Eastern Standard/Daylight Saving Time. I live on the West Coast, therefore, I need to ensure I have delivered the project by 9 PM my time, which is Pacific Standard/Daylight Saving Time. If in doubt, go onto the freelance website. They have a clock set to EST/EDT.

Milestones

Large projects can be broken down into what is known as *milestones*. Say you have a project for 50 articles, and your client wants 25 delivered each week on Fridays.

You can set up the two separate delivery dates—*milestones*—with a description of what is to be delivered (25 articles) under *terms and conditions*.

This is common practice, as some projects are for large quantities of content. I have worked on projects for 150 articles, which have been broken down into six week segments of 25 articles per week.

Escrow

Escrow is one of the reasons I recommend you bid on *fixed price* projects. Clients must deposit the agreed upon amount into an *escrow* system. In other words, the freelance website holds the money in trust for you until you deliver the project to the client.

Never, ever, write one word until the full sum is deposited into *escrow*. If the client has accepted your *terms and conditions* and a few days pass without *escrow* funding, send the client a message informing them you cannot begin work until *escrow* is funded and the delivery date is in jeopardy. This usually jolts the client into action.

Without Milestones

If the project has one delivery date without *milestones*, the entire amount must be deposited into escrow.

With Milestones

If the project is broken into *milestones*, the client need only deposit the *milestone* amount into *escrow*. If your proposal of $1,000 for those 50 articles has been accepted by the client and the project is broken into two delivery dates, the client must deposit $500 immediately for the first delivery date.

After you meet the first delivery date, immediately

request *escrow* on the next *milestone* or final delivery date. Again, do not work on the project until *escrow* is funded.

Should you bid on hourly projects, be aware there is a risk you might end up holding an unpaid invoice in your hand with little recourse. There are several conditions attached to protection from deadbeat clients and, if you qualify, there is a cap to compensation.

Private Invitations

After you have established yourself, you may be the recipient of *private invitations*. The *private invitation* might be from a client you have worked for in the past, or it might be a result of the client searching the keywords you included in your profile.

You receive an email notification of the *private invitation*. You can follow the link provided to either put forth a proposal in the normal fashion as described in Chapter 17 or deny the request. If you deny, the system gives a number of options to inform the client why you are denying the invitation.

Invoicing

Freelance bid websites have billing systems, which saves you the effort of preparing invoices. This is one of the features I like the most.

A few clicks and notification is sent to the client for release of *escrow* and invoices are generated for your records.

Commission Fees

Freelance bid websites stay in business by collecting *commission* based on a percentage of the total project amount. The amount of the *commission* depends upon your membership.

Freelance websites differ in the way they charge *commission fees*. Some charge the freelancers; others charge the clients. For the websites that charge the freelancers, there is a way around paying commission fees. You quite simply work the amount into your proposal figure, as I show you in the next chapter.

Forums

Freelance bid websites have *Forums* where freelancers can ask questions or discuss issues. *Forums* can be a time-suck, or they can be helpful.

You can search for an answer or ask a question. Questions are answered by other freelancers, with occasional input by administrative staff. The problem with freelancers answering questions is they often bring their own "baggage" into the answer. This is where the time-suck occurs—wading through the muck to find a practical answer, if one exists.

I rarely use the *Forums*. I prefer to find my answers in the guidelines. If the guidelines do not answer my question clearly, I contact support representatives directly with my question. Support typically returns my email within 24 hours, and the representatives are helpful, patient, and go the extra mile to sort out your issue. It is to their benefit; you are their bread and butter.

The one situation where *forums* provide information that support representatives do not is rogue clients. I have seen more than one thread warning freelancers off certain clients who dodge releasing escrow, are difficult to work with, demand more than the initial project scope without further compensation, or leave unwarranted poor reviews.

Dispute Resolution

Dispute resolution services may be available if problems arise between clients and freelancers. The most common problem is payment. As their policies differ, I cover this topic in Chapters 17 and 20.

Blacklisted

This is what happens if you work off-site at either the instigation of a prospective or current client or through your initiative:

You are banned permanently and prohibited from working on their sites.

That is it. No second chances.

Freelance bid websites have identification verification procedures to ensure their freelancers are exactly who they promote—professionals. There is zero chance of sneaking back under another identity.

As a last note: I have noticed a trend where freelancers are posting their skills as projects. In essence, it is not a paying gig. Make sure you carefully read the project description to avoid bidding on someone's self-promotion project. I am at somewhat of a loss to understand why freelancers are doing this as clients are not perusing project lists. A heads-up tip to avoid wasting bids.

Quick Summary
- Freelance bid websites are platforms where clients post projects for writers to place bid
- Exercise great caution to avoid petty-pay content mills and scams
- Choose the *Writing & Translation* category under the work tab
- Search *fixed price* projects at least twice daily to place bids promptly

- Choose projects based on expertise, favorable locations, and the competition
- Bid on numerous projects until your schedule is full
- Do not overextend yourself by accepting too many projects
- Double-check *terms and conditions* before accepting
- Project deadlines are typically 12 AM EST/EDT
- Large projects can be broken into *milestones* for manageability
- Do not begin work on a project until *escrow* is funded in full
- *Private invitations* are projects clients create for individual writers
- Clients can take screenshots of you on hourly rate projects
- Freelance bid websites generate invoices
- Freelance bid websites charge *commission fees*
- *Forums* can be helpful or unproductive time sucks
- *Dispute resolution* may be available
- Never work off-site

Next up: how to leverage your skills to your advantage.

CHAPTER 16
LEVERAGE YOUR SKILLS

"To establish oneself in the world, one has to do all one can to appear established."
~ [Duc de] La Rochefoucauld, Maxims, 1678

The next big boost you make to your profile page to make yourself attractive to prospective clients is through *skills tests*. Freelance bid websites offer numerous tests, some of which are free and others that charge.

Skills tests demonstrate your knowledge and enhance your chances of obtaining that all-important first project. It also helps your rank (to be covered in later chapters).

Before you begin the test, be sure to read the details to understand exactly what the test consists of. Be aware all the tests are time limited. Scores are available after you have completed the test. Should you fail or obtain a low score, make that test invisible on your profile page if permissible. Typically, you can retake tests after a waiting period.

At the very least, I recommend you take the following tests. You can do them gradually over time:

Article Writing	Grammar
Blogs	Non-fiction writing
Content Writing	Online writing

Copywriting	Proofreading
Creative Writing	Punctuation/Spelling
Editing	Web Writing
Ghostwriting	Word Processing

Your objective is to obtain high scores placing you in the top percentages in a given category. That percentage fluctuates as other freelance writers take the same test.

Your percentage may decrease or increase dependent on how others score on their tests. This is out of your control. Do not stress overmuch if your score decreases. That decrease can turn into an increase. The end goal is to show you have taken the tests.

Bilingualism is another fantastic asset. Fluency in another language opens up opportunities. Take the relevant skills translation test. Translation into your mother tongue is best, as it is believed a person has better cultural and linguistic understanding involving their first language. Translating into your second language lacks these two elements, as you are constantly learning the language and may not have been immersed in the environment where the language is spoken. If you have special skills from life experience, such as legal, medical, financial, newsletters, reports, resumes, sales, academic, press releases, speeches or user guides, take those tests as well.

Each site has more than one category for skills tests. If you have experience and knowledge in any of the different categories, review the tests under that category to discover if there are other tests you can successfully write.

This sounds like a lot of work and time consuming, but you definitely reap benefits from investment in *skills tests*. You can still bid on projects while you are writing *skills tests*.

Every slight edge you gain over your competition is invaluable. There is a multitude of freelance writers competing in the same project pool. *Skills tests* just might put you ahead of the crowd.

Quick Summary
- *Skills tests* boost your profile page's attractiveness
- *Skills tests* demonstrate your knowledge
- *Skills tests* enhance the possibilities of obtaining projects
- Results will fluctuate
- Read instructions carefully
- Tests are timed
- Take all relevant *skills tests*

Our next chapter is focused on writing a standout proposal to win projects. Here goes...

CHAPTER 17
HOW TO WRITE A STANDOUT PROPOSAL

"The first step in exceeding your customer's expectations is to know those expectations."
~ Roy H. Williams, Author & Marketing Consultant

You now have the knowledge and information required to begin bidding on projects. The last element—and, perhaps, the most important—is the proposal letter.

This is where you sell your abilities, and why you are the best freelancer for a project. A well-written proposal letter cements your attributes to convince the client you, indeed, are the best choice.

Each proposal should be customized to the project. Clients are often savvy enough to know when you are using a generic proposal letter and generally pass you by.

Write a professional proposal. In other words, do not use clichés and smarmy phrasing. You want to be taken seriously, rather than sounding like a used-car salesperson.

Incomplete Project Description Proposal

I have chosen a project description that does not include enough information to nail down a quote to illustrate how to respond in your proposal:

I am looking for a fluent in English content writer that can help create legitimate content for my law websites. I have 4 in total, and would also like assistance in updating and maintaining a blog as well. Proficient in English is a must, and some legal knowledge is also a plus.

This is a proposal I would write in response:

Hello — *(the full name of the client is never given so it is impossible to personally direct the proposal)*

I am a Native English speaker proficient in both US and UK versions.

I am an experienced freelance writer, editor, proofreader, and fiction and nonfiction author.

I am detail-oriented, with high standards of professionalism. My grammar and spelling skills are excellent.

I am experienced in producing high-quality legal content. As a former paralegal of twenty years, I have extensive real-life knowledge and expertise in the legal fields of matrimonial, personal injury (Plaintiff and Defense), corporate, commercial, and wills and estates. I have written hundreds of malpractice articles for US attorneys.

I attach a selection of samples for your review, which demonstrate the caliber of my research and writing abilities. I also attach my resume and testimonials for your review.

Your project description indicates you require legal content for 4 websites, as well

DARLENE ELIZABETH WILLIAMS

as maintaining a blog. In order to provide you with a fair quote, would you please provide the following information:

1. Area of law
2. Number of articles required
3. Number of words per article
4. Number of blog posts per month
5. Length of blog posts
6. Timeline for provision of articles and blog posts.

I have placed a nominal bid of $25 for the project, which I will revise accordingly upon receipt of further details.

All work is processed through Copyscape for duplicate content and DupeFree Pro for keyword density (if required) prior to delivery.

To avoid possible misunderstandings, please advise prior to release of escrow if revisions are required. Once escrow is released, no further revisions are provided.

I am honest, reliable, meet deadlines, and strive to produce quality content to your satisfaction.

I look forward to receipt of the requested information, so I may finalize my proposal.

Thank you for the opportunity to bid on your project.

Yours,

Darlene Elizabeth Williams

Stating you will revise your fee upon receipt of further details is in your best interests. Many freelancers bid on projects without understanding the full scope of a project, only to be unpleasantly surprised when the client hands

134

over a project which far exceeds the amount of work anticipated. All of a sudden, a respectable sum of money for work becomes a losing proposition. You can turn down the project, but rejecting awarded projects may have negative connotations on your reputation in the future.

Recently, I submitted a proposal asking for further details to provide a concrete quote. Upon receipt of the material, I sent the client a detailed message listing all the tasks associated—with my reasons why these tasks were necessary—with the project. I then quoted triple the amount of my "placer bid". I convinced the client in the message that the work was required. He accepted my bid and awarded me the project. It took about two weeks of back-and-forth, but it was worth it in the end.

Complete Project Description Proposal

Next is a project description I can respond to with a quote included:

> *I am looking for a fluent in English content writer that can help create legitimate content for my general law practice websites. I have 4 in total, and would also like assistance in updating and maintaining a blog as well. I need 16 articles of 500 words for the websites and 4 articles of 350 words per month for the blog. Proficient in English is a must, and some legal knowledge is also a plus. Please type "Dragon" at the top of your proposal so I know you've read the entire job description.*

Hello — Dragon.
I am a Native English speaker proficient in both US and UK versions.
I am an experienced freelance writer,

editor, proofreader, and fiction and nonfiction author.

I am detail-oriented, with high standards of professionalism. My grammar and spelling skills are excellent.

I am experienced in producing high-quality legal content. As a former paralegal of twenty years, I have extensive real-life knowledge and expertise in the legal fields of matrimonial, personal injury (Plaintiff and Defense), corporate, commercial, and wills and estates. I have written hundreds of malpractice articles for US attorneys.

I attach a selection of samples for your review, which demonstrate the caliber of my research and writing abilities. I have also attached my resume and testimonials for your review.

My bid $z [total of $x + $y] encompasses 16 articles of 500 words each and 4 blog posts of 350 words each (x), plus commission fees (y). I have indicated a delivery date of two weeks to ensure you receive superior content.

All work is processed through Copyscape for duplicate content and DupeFree Pro for keyword density (if required) prior to delivery.

To avoid possible misunderstandings, please advise prior to release of escrow if revisions are required. Once escrow is released, no further revisions are provided.

I am honest, reliable, meet deadlines, and strive to produce quality content to your satisfaction.

Thank you for the opportunity to bid on your project.

Yours,

Darlene Elizabeth Williams

Several clients request you type a special code word written in the job description at the top of your proposal. They request the code word to ensure you have read the entire job description in the hopes of lessening the number of unqualified applicants.

Run—Don't Walk—Job Descriptions

And now for a downright wacky project description:

.....copywriter............copywriter.....
.....copywriter............copywriter.....
.....copywriter............copywriter.....
.....copywriter............copywriter.....

Seven hours after posting this "job", the client has received zero proposals. Wonder why? Most definitely not worth wasting bids to define this job description.

I keep a proposal letter template on my computer, which I pull up and fill in the blanks, add pertinent information (i.e. I was a legal assistant) that appeals to the client, and include a summary of the job description so the client understands I have read the entire project details.

Delivery Date

You are required to indicate a *delivery date* along with your proposal. Unless you are extremely fast and accurate, give yourself the appropriate amount of time to research, write, and edit the articles. The most important goal is to provide the client with excellent content, so he returns with more work and/or leaves you a five star review.

The client might ask you if you can shorten your *delivery date*. If possible, agree to an earlier *delivery date*.

If you are loaded with work, advise you are fully booked and x number of days or weeks is the earliest date you can deliver.

Elements of a Proposal Letter

Your proposal should be succinct and to the point. Clients are wading through 30-40-50 or more applicants in some cases. State your qualifications, experience, services, and proposed fee concisely or risk the client moving onto another applicant because of time restrictions.

The proposal letters I write work well for me. You might feel you want to express yourself with different wording. That is perfectly acceptable. Just remember to include the following elements:

- Write the code word at the top if requested
- Identify you are a Native English speaker
- State your expertise
- If you have work experience or life experience with the topic, provide this information to the client
- Repeat the project description so the client knows you read the entire project listing
- Always upload samples (these are from your portfolio you created on Constant Content or, if you have worked previous similar projects, samples contained in your files or portfolios)
- Include a complete breakdown of how you have arrived at your fees
- Assure the client the content is plagiarism-free
- State whether and when revisions are offered. Limit yourself to offering two revisions. Inform the client revisions are available until such-and-such a date (i.e. one week after delivery). You do not want the client showing up like a bad penny a month later when you are deep into writing other

projects.

- Always thank the client for the opportunity to bid on their project.

Pricing

Submitting a monetary figure for the project is a bit stressful. You want to be paid fairly for the project, but it is anyone's guess how much money the client is willing to pay.

For your first jobs, be prepared to be paid less than your optimal fees. You are on the bottom rung of the ladder. As you gather projects and reviews in your writing arsenal, raise your fees to what you feel is fair.

Estimate the time it will take you to research, write, and edit the project. If the topic is familiar, it will take you less time. If it is a subject new to you or complex, take that into consideration.

Sometimes a client is searching for the lowest price. That is their mindset and nothing will change it. If you lose out on a project awarded to a freelancer charging a ridiculously low price, shrug your shoulders and say to yourself, "You get what you pay for." Even though you know the client is going to receive a lousy return for their pittance payment, that is their problem, not yours.

There have been occasions where a client has accepted a pittance proposal, received the work, been horrified, and contacted me to redo the work for my price. You just never know.

Samples

I have two standard documents I always upload: my resume and testimonials from clients. You can take a snippet or sentences from previous client reviews, paste them into a word document, and call it *Testimonials*.

Customize your work samples to the job description. If

you do not have samples that exactly reflect the work requested, try to choose samples close in nature.

If possible, try to include three samples. At a minimum, you should upload no less than two. Attaching more than three samples is pointless, as the client probably will not read more than the three. There is no purpose to inundating a client with samples. The three articles will be skimmed at best.

Quick Summary

- Proposals are your sales letters
- Customize your proposal for each project
- Keep proposals succinct
- State if you are a Native English speaker
- List your expertise
- Provide relevant experience information
- Repeat project description
- Breakdown fees and commission charges
- Inform the client of your revisions policy
- Thank the client for consideration of your proposal
- Upload samples
- Submit your fees based on research, writing, and editing time required
- Choose a delivery date

This is it! The last tool for bidding on projects is the proposal letter. The next chapter is an overview of Elance. And, then, you are set to begin bidding and earning money. After all, this is what it is all about: earning money in a professional occupation you are passionate about.

CHAPTER 18
ELANCE OVERVIEW

"When a person with money meets a person with experience, the person with experience will get the money. And the person with money will get some experience."

~ Leonard Lauder, February 1985

First tasks first. You need to complete a 100 percent profile on Elance. We have already discussed most of the tasks involved in setting up your profile in Chapter 12.

Register

Type Elance in your browser. Click on the blue *Register Now (it's free)* button. This takes you to *Create an Account*. Click on *I Want to Work*. Fill in the required boxes. Note: You must use your legal name for Elance verification. Your profile shows your first name. You have the option of whether your full surname or initial is displayed.

Fill in all the information and click on the green *Register* at the bottom. Now you choose your category. In your case, it is *Writing and Translation*.

Once that is complete, you are taken to your home screen called *My Elance*, which looks like this (with the exception of a green bar for your profile completeness):

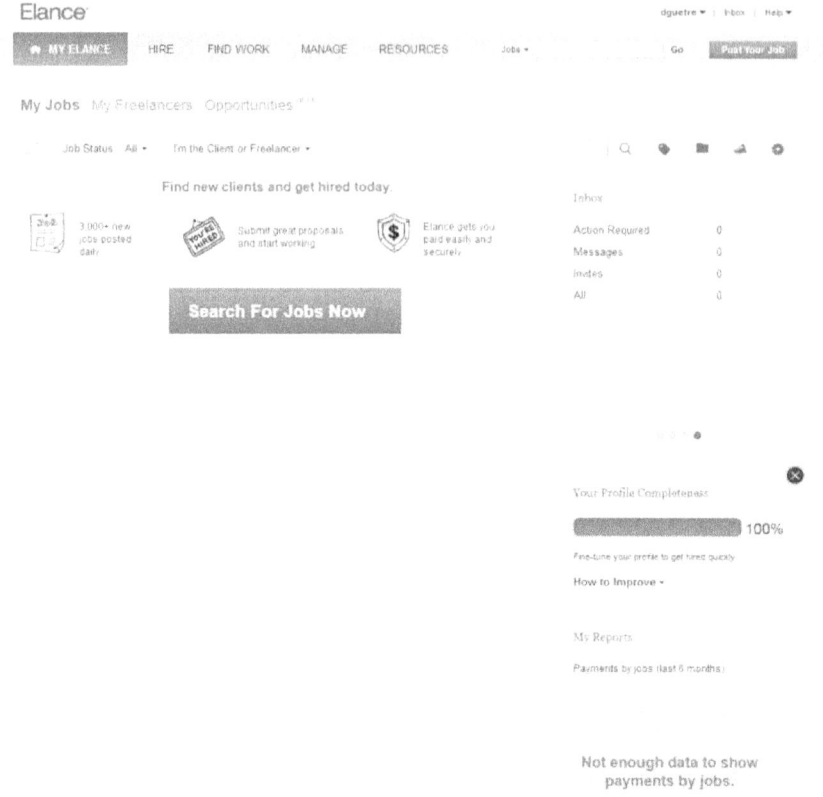

At the top you will see the following tabs:
- My Elance
- Hire
- Find Work
- Manage
- Resources

In the upper right corner is your name, inbox, and help.

Membership

You may have heard you should never pay membership fees. I agree with this philosophy in general, but there are good reasons why I urge you to purchase a membership on Elance. With a membership, you gain access to additional projects and what I generically call "bids". Your monthly membership provides you with a specific amount of bids. For instance, my *Individual* membership on Elance provides me with 60 bids per month, with an option to purchase further bids if need be. Every project you submit a proposal for reduces your monthly allotment of bids. The number of bids required to submit a proposal can vary depending on whether it is a client-sponsored project, the allocated budget, and if you choose to sponsor your own proposal.

The *Individual* plan is a nominal monthly fee and pays for itself. The *Individual* plan permits:

- access to all jobs within the *Writing and Translation* category
- adding bids if you need them
- appearing higher in search results
- adding categories
- viewing competitors' pricing
- showcasing samples in your proposals
- free transfer of money to your PayPal account.

Click on your name at the top right-hand corner of the *My Elance* page and, then, on *Membership* to select the *Individual* plan.

Building a Superb Profile Page

Under the tab *Find Work* is a subtab: *Freelance Profile*. Click on this subtab and you are ready to create a hundred percent complete freelance profile.

On the top left-hand corner, there is a box where you upload your professional headshot.

On the sidebar of your profile page there are the following tabs:

Overview

This is where you fill in your first and last name. Check the box if you only want your last initial displayed.

Now you need a great tagline. This is not optional. You want to be succinct, but still give the client the full scope of what it is you do. My tagline is "Exceptional Editing Services; Reasonable Rates".

Inputting an hourly rate is optional, but I do include my rate. The first box is where you state your rate; the second box is where Elance automatically calculates your rate, plus Elance fees (more on this later).

If you have a YouTube video insert the URL in the next box. I do not have a video, but I am considering doing a short snippet for my website and freelance sites.

Your profile description is entered into the *Overview* box. You are limited to a certain number of characters. You may have to edit this somewhat if it is quite long. This is where you want to shine. It is the first piece of information clients read on your profile page. The first two sentences of your overview appears next to your name when you submit a proposal. Make those two sentences really count.

Service Description is the next box. Tell prospective clients how you will provide them with stellar service. Speak about how you handle your work assignments: you meet deadlines; you communicate with clients; you tailor the work to their specifications; you are organized; you are amenable to milestones. Make a prospect feel like they are unique and will be treated as such.

For payment terms, I say, "Payment terms, turnaround time, and all other details to be confirmed at the time of acceptance of project." This is standard. I have never had a quibble with a client over this statement.

Keywords is the final box on this screen. You are allowed up to 15 keywords. Think carefully about the keywords. If you were a client, what keywords would you use to search for a freelancer for your writing project? What are your skills? What is your expertise?

Now click *Save*. Ensure your country and local time are correct underneath your tagline on your profile page.

Job History

This page is empty, of course, but soon you shall have an impressive list of past projects. A rectangular box at the top of the page shows:

- Your *Level*
- how many jobs and *milestones* you completed
- how many reviews you received
- your recommendation percentage
- how many clients you worked for
- your percentage of repeat clients
- lifetime earnings
- average earnings per client

Levels are calculated by Elance based on your statistics for:

- Client Relationship
- Earnings
- Positive Reviews

Your *Level* will be 1. As your statistics improve by completing projects, you accumulate points which determines your level. The better your stats, obviously the higher your ranking.

Underneath this box is a list of all your projects, with reviews, ratings, and feedback from clients.

Portfolio

To upload the articles you wrote for Constant Content and any other writing samples you have, click on *Edit Portfolio*. When you upload a sample, give it a title, describe what you did, and input tags. Under *Advanced Options* you can put a collection of content into sets. If the sample content is online, you can add the URL. Do not forget to save! It is frustrating to repeat the whole process again.

Once you have uploaded all your samples, you can organize where you want them to appear in the list under the *More Options* menu.

You can forward your profile to friends and potential clients by clicking the *Forward Profile* link.

Skills

Remember Chapter 13 on skills tests? This is where you put yourself to the test. Click on *Add Skills* and choose from the predetermined list. Do not limit yourself when choosing your skills. Add every skill possible. At the top right, there is a link *View Available Tests*.

If you do well, it is listed for clients to see. If you do not score well, you can hide the score and try again in 14 days. Skills tests are free and invaluable. If you have test rankings anywhere from the Top 30% and up, it is displayed in green. That is what you are aiming for, even if you have to retake a test.

If you are below the Top 30%, you receive a green checkmark. Skills rank you higher in searches for freelancers.

Resume/C.V.

The first portion of the screen contains your *Overview information* and *Service Description*. Below this, you add your *Certifications, Licenses, and Education* by clicking on the *Add* button. You are prompted to fill in the information.

You add your *Education* underneath. Anything goes as long as it is relevant to an expertise you are claiming. If your expertise is pets and you have taken a grooming course, include it.

At the top right, there is an *Add Reference* button. You can highlight previous projects and clients outside of Elance. I include every project I have completed.

Contact Info

Under *Contact Information* your first and last name and address are mandatory. Optional is your title, email address, phone and fax numbers, website URL, and Instant Messaging. You manage what further information is visible on your *Profile* page.

On the left side of the *Contact Information* screen you set your *Privacy* settings. The only box you should check is *Do not publicly display my earnings as a freelancer on Elance (Only show to clients within proposals)*. If you check any other boxes, you limit your visibility to clients.

Communications settings are a personal preference. There is no right or wrong, but I would advise you set your communications to receive notifications for job opportunities and Elance newsletters.

Billing and Payment requires your legal name and address for invoices. It is your responsibility to determine whether you are legally required by your country to complete a W-9 or provide a Value Added Tax (VAT) identification number.

Client and Job Preferences permits you to set your availability and client and job criteria via options in the dropdown menus.

Private talent cloud is not applicable to individual freelancers.

ID Verification

Elance offers individual freelancers the opportunity to

verify their identification. A verification service contacts you via Skype after you provide the following:

- Thumbnail photo on your profile
- Government issued ID
- Skype account (most current version)
- Webcam and microphone for the verification interview

The process of *verification identification* is explained in full here. My ID has been verified, as this completes my profile 100 percent.

Verified Credentials

Verified credentials may be of value when clients are reviewing proposals. It is a method of certifying you actually earned a certificate, diploma, or degree, or your past employment is valid.

There is a cost attached: US citizens pay $15 per credential; international freelancers pay $25 per credential.

The process of credential verification is explained in full here. I have not verified my credentials as I am not convinced paying money for verification is warranted. I personally feel my Elance work history and references suffice; however, should you feel your degree would assist you immensely, please do verify it.

Now you have completely filled out all of your Elance profile, we are going to go back to your home page: *My Elance*.

My Elance

Your home page is devoid of much information at this point. As you have not yet applied for any jobs, the center of the screen consists of a large green button *Search for Jobs Now*.

But, before you do that, let us become familiar with the home page as it is the central location for your information.

To the right is your *Inbox*, which lists:

Action Required   0
Messages   0
Invites   0
All   0

That changes once you apply for projects.

Underneath the *Inbox*, you can view trends. I am not a fan of trends as I said in Chapter 13 about Constant Content. Chasing trends can be a waste of time, unless you happen to have an expertise in what is trending.

Your *Profile Completeness* has a green bar with a percentage next to it. Ideally, it says 100 percent.

My Reports shows payments by jobs for the last six months. You have not worked on Elance yet, so there is a message "Not enough data to show payments by job." That also changes once you work on projects.

Finally, *Open Jobs* lists your current projects. It is your ultimate goal to obtain open jobs.

Your home page is a screenshot of all activity associated with your account.

Now we dig a little deeper.

Find Work Tab

You can ignore the tab at the top that says *Hire*. The next tab *Find Work* will get a workout from you over the years. There are seven categories under *Find Work* and I will go through each individually.

1. Search Jobs

This is it! This is where you put into action everything you have learned thus far and, especially, Chapter 14 explaining how freelance bid websites operate. Scoot back to the subsection How to Locate Projects if necessary.

Vetting Clients

Before you submit proposals, we need to talk about vetting clients. It is a vital process to success. Eliminating clients with a small award percentage rate or pay abysmal rates saves you money (by not spending bids) and time when you could be making a proposal on a better prospect.

Elance places the client's name and location at the bottom line of the short job description located in the search function. So, for instance, if you search *Find Work; Search Jobs; Writing & Translation; Article Writing* you receive results for all jobs in that category. These are the short job descriptions. For full length job descriptions and details, you need to click on the condensed job description. More on full length job descriptions later.

For now, we are concentrating on vetting clients. The bottom line shows four circles with a dollar sign in the first circle. The circles may be grey or some or all of them colored green.

If all the circles are grey, this means the client either has not awarded any projects or is a new client to Elance.

Green circles mean the client has awarded one or more projects. The more green circles, the higher number of projects awarded.

Hover your mouse over the circles and a pop-up box appears. The following snapshot information appears in the box:
- Name of client
- Total Purchased with a dollar figure
- Payment Verified
- Percentage of projects awarded vs the number

of projects posted
- Member Since: with date noted
- Location: where in the world the client is located

What you are looking for is a project with green circles (the more the better), a client who is payment verified, who awards a high percentage of posted projects, and their location.

I selected two projects as examples to illustrate the above. They were both article writing projects.

The first project has two green circles, total purchased $84, payment is verified, 29% awarded (2 of 7 projects), a member since April 2012, and located in the United Kingdom.

The second project has three green circles, total purchased is between $500—$5K, payment is verified, 89% awarded (17 of 19 projects), a member since April 2012, and located in the United States.

Just looking at the statistics should be an indication of which project is the better of the two. The second client has a higher rate of awarding projects and has spent substantially more money than the first, although they both became members in April 2012.

The first client has awarded two projects paying $84. Let us assume and divide that number by two, for a total of $42 per project. In the short description, I read this client wants ten articles of 500 words each. That is 5,000 words. Divide $42 by 5,000. The pay rate is $0.008 per word. Not even one cent per word. And, of course, they want stellar researched and written articles. This is the type of client and project you do not want to waste your bids on.

The second project owner sounds enticing. They award the majority of their projects and spend a fair bit of money. There is just one last safety check. Check out *their* references. Click on their name and it takes you to the client's *Client info*.

Client info shows the ratings the clients have given for all the projects awarded. Not every project has a rating, but you can still reasonably assess the client's reputation. Next to the rating, there is an area where the freelancer can provide a response. Here is where you find out if the client was accessible, clear with instructions, and easy or difficult to work with. The odd time there are freelancers warning you off the client. I would take the warning seriously and move on. You might have to scroll through a number of pages to get a clear idea about the client.

Submitting a Proposal

When you locate the first project you feel is appropriate for your talents, you are going to submit a proposal. You should have your proposal letter template ready for customization.

You have clicked on the job description. To your right is *Create Your Proposal*. Plug in your customized proposal letter. Underneath is a box *Outline your approach to the job; or ask for more info*. Precisely detail what information (if any) you need to complete your proposal, and succinctly describe your methods for completion of the project.

It is advisable to add samples to your proposal. You can upload from your computer or your *account file*. Every document I upload from my computer I add to my *account file* to save the hassle of locating and uploading for each proposal.

You have the option of proposing milestones. Personally, I do not add milestones until I have been awarded the project and the client has informed me of a deadline. Most times, when the project is awarded, the client provides this information.

For *Cost & Timing,* enter your fee in the *My Earnings* box. Elance automatically calculates the amount *Billed to Client* to include their fees. Finally, select an *Estimated Delivery Date* from the dropdown menu.

Connects Required tells you how many connects (aka bids) are required to apply for the project. You can use additional connects to place your bid in the top three proposals. Elance only permits three sponsored proposals.

Preview your proposal and carefully reread it. It is surprising how often you find an error. Your brain is often working faster than your fingers when you write proposals. Once you are satisfied, click *submit*.

After you submit your proposal, a *Status* box appears above your proposal, which offers you the opportunity to update or withdraw your proposal.

Your proposal is now complete. You can search for other projects or, if you have jobs on the go, work on them while you wait to see if the client accepts your proposal.

2. Browse

The *Browse* screen merely categorizes the job categories with links to select subcategories. In my opinion, *Browse* does not contain enough subcategories and it is better to use *Search Jobs* so you can check several subcategories.

3. Opportunities

This feature lists projects recommended by Elance. I have yet to find a recommendation that fits my expertise. You can scan through the recommendations, but it is not a valuable feature in my opinion.

4. *My Stats*

My Stats details your statistics for *Service Delivery, Client Relationships*, and *Marketing*. These statistics are used to determine your *Level*.

The top of the screen shows your category—*Writing and Translations*—with your current *Level*, how many points you need to advance to the next *Level*, points accumulated during the past week, and your *rank* in comparison to all of the freelancers in your category.

There is a *trend chart* you can click on, which has graphs that illustrate your points and earnings for the past six months.

There are three major sections on *My Stats*:

- *Service Delivery* — details your six month earnings; jobs with feedback; earnings percentage; and *milestones* completed. It also lists violations and cancellations, which detract from your service delivery stats.
- *Client Relationship* — lists client recommendation percentage; earnings per client; number of clients; and number of repeat clients.
- *Marketing* — sets out your six month bookings; job accept rate percentage; invite response rates; tested skills; and verified credentials. If you propose below the client's stated budget on proposals, it has a negative impact on your marketing statistics and *Level* ranking.

The page is helpful as it shows where you can improve different aspects of your approach to proposals and completion of projects. Obviously, you want to rank as high as possible. If you find you have a low job accept rate percentage, perhaps you might not be targeting the right projects, providing appropriate portfolio samples, or you might need to tweak your *profile*, *proposals*, or *outlines*.

To the right of these sections is a box that details your activity in comparison to all freelancers in your *Level*.

I visit this page often to review my statistics to determine whether I need a different approach to projects.

5. *Freelancer Profile*

Freelancer profile is just that: your *Profile*. You can edit your *Profile* via this link.

6. *Proposal Requests*

Proposal Requests lists *private invitations* from clients. When you receive an email notifying you of a *private invitation*, do not ignore it! Either accept by submitting a proposal or decline. If you decide to decline, there is a dropdown menu with several options for you to choose.

Ignoring *private invitations* from clients penalizes you in accumulating points for your next *Level*.

7. *Watch List*

You can add jobs or clients to your *Watch List*. I do not recommend adding a job posting to your *Watch List*. Either apply for the project immediately or pass it by. Adding it to your *Watch List* accomplishes nothing of benefit. You are basically watching other freelancers apply for that job.

Adding clients is a different matter. Every time a favored client on your *Watch List* posts a job, it appears in your *Watch List*. This means you have less chance of missing out on the posting altogether. I definitely recommend adding clients.

Manage Tab

Now we are going to move over to the next tab: *Manage*. This the tab you use for the financial aspects of your projects; in other words, receiving payment and tracking payments and commission fees.

1. Payments

Payments is a payments list which you can filter up to the previous 90 days. You can narrow your search down to:
- By date range
- By PO number
- All unpaid invoices
- All paid invoices
- All partially paid invoices
- All not funded
- All funded
- All not released
- All released
- All pending

This is a quick system of determining whether escrow has been funded, released, or is pending. You do not want to start work on a project that is not funded—you can check if it has here. If the project is listed as pending, do not start work. This means the client's credit card has not yet been authenticated and escrow is not in place.

Likewise, if a release of escrow has been sent and the client has not taken the appropriate actions, you need to follow up with the client. If the funds are released, you can withdraw them (this is done through a subtab under Manage).

2. Send Status Reports

Elance requires freelancers to send Status Reports to clients by 12:00 AM Eastern Time each Sunday. The Status Report informs the client:

- whether the project is progressing well
- if there are problems that need to be addressed so you can continue to work on the project
- what was accomplished during the week
- what the client can expect you to work on during the upcoming week

It is important to send Status Reports on time. If they are late or missed, you are docked points which impacts your Level. Ensure you add Status Reports to your scheduling to avoid penalties.

All current projects are listed under the Send Status Reports and the date on which the reports are due. It is a simple process that takes approximately five minutes. To create a Status Report, go to the Manage tab and click on Create at the far right.

3. Billing

Billing is similar to Payments in that you can view your billing list by:

- Date range
- PO number
- All unpaid invoices
- All paid invoices
- All partially paid invoices
- All not funded
- All funded
- All not released
- All released
- All pending

...for up to the previous 45 days.

4. Files

Files are a list of your account files, which you added to your account when uploading your samples to proposals. You can access your Portfolio from this tab as well.

If you wish to add files to your account, substitute a revision, download, or delete, click Options next to each document's name.

5. Financial Accounts

This tab has the various methods of withdrawing or making payments—PayPal, bank account if you are a US resident, prepaid Payoneer Mastercard (outside US only), and Skrill (outside US only). Plug in your PayPal information or other financial information. It may take up to five days for PayPal and bank account information to appear.

6. Transactions

This page has your entire transaction history with Elance. Each payment for membership dues, invoices created by Elance for the clients, and project fee invoices are available for either viewing or downloading. This page is your best friend for Elance accounting purposes.

7. Withdraw Funds

My favorite page. This is the payday page. Here you withdraw funds to your preset preference under Financial Accounts. It takes up to two days for the money to transfer from Elance to your account.

8. My Team

My Team consists of you. There is nothing you need to do on this page as you are the only team member.

9. My Reports

My Reports lists all payments made by freelancers. This will not apply to you as you will not incur ancillary costs for writing projects. Supplies such as paper, pens, printer ink, etc., are overhead costs. The only time you might issue a purchase order to recoup expenses paid out-of-pocket is if the client asks you to purchase a particular book. I have never had this occur.

Resources Tab

Onto the last tab: *Resources*. I am not going to go into detail about the subtabs as it is discretionary whether you use any of the features. In all honesty, I have never used any of them, although you may find the videos under Elance University useful:

- Elance University
- Trust & Safety
- Blog
- Water Cooler
- Referral Program
- Widgets & Tools
- Partner Offers
- My apps

I feel my time is better spent applying for projects than hanging around a virtual water cooler.

We have explored how to get around on Elance and find the tools and features you require. Now we need to discuss what happens when you are awarded a project.

I won! I won!

You received an email notification that a client has selected your proposal and awarded you the project. Once the feeling of jubilation settles down, there is work to be done. But do take time to congratulate yourself. You earned it.

Your first task is to accept the project. Go to my *My Jobs* page and click on *Finalizing Terms*. Next, go to your home screen *My Elance* (second tab from the left at the top). Under the project name, click *Review Terms*. Both you and the client have to accept the *terms* before the project award is complete. If the client has already included *terms* that are acceptable, you need merely click *Accept*, then *Submit*.

If you wish to modify any of the *terms*—fees, delivery, milestones—you can do so and submit them for the client's review. The client accepts, modifies, or rejects your modifications. Do not hesitate to use the message board to communicate with the client about *terms*. If you are dissatisfied with any of the *terms*, explain your reasons, your suggested modifications, and ask if the client is amenable to your changes.

Elance charges 8.75 percent commission across the board, regardless of the type of membership you have. In the past, the freelancer used to pay the commission; now, it can be included in the terms and conditions so that the client pays.

Be absolutely sure the Elance commission fees are included in the *escrow deposit terms* before you click *accept*. I missed that on a project not long ago, and ended up paying $80 to Elance myself rather than the client paying the fees.

When *terms* are accepted by both sides and the full amount (including Elance fees) has been deposited into *escrow*, you can begin work on your project.

Elance allows you to communicate with the client via

Skype, telephone, and email. My advice is to communicate with clients only via Elance's message board. My reason for this is simple: should a dispute arise, the issue is documented on Elance's system. You cannot prove or disprove what was said over Skype or telephone.

Keep in mind you need to submit *Status Reports* every Sunday by midnight Eastern Time.

Projects without Milestones

Once the project is awarded and accepted, a *Workroom* is created under the project description. You enter a *Workroom* via your *My Elance* tab and clicking on the project description.

Projects without *milestones* are simple as far as delivery and payment are concerned. Let us say your project is for twenty articles due within a week. *Escrow* is deposited, *terms* are agreed upon, and you are working on the project. If the delivery date falls on any day of the week other than a Sunday, you must still file a *status report*.

Your delivery date has arrived and you are ready to hand the articles over to the client and request *release of escrow*. There are different approaches you can take to deliver the articles and request *release of escrow* funds, but using a *status report* is the most efficient.

On your home screen *My Elance* where your proposals and jobs are located, click on the *Actions* dropdown menu. Choose *status reports* and *create* a new *status report.* Use the dropdown menu on the *status report* to mark the project as *complete*, upload the articles, and type a "thank you" note in the comments box at the bottom of the screen. Hit the green *submit* button, and it is sent to the client immediately.

At this time, Elance automatically creates an invoice for your records, and sends a *Request for Release* (of *escrow* funds) to the client. The client has a maximum of thirty days to release the funds or Elance automatically releases them to you. If the client has not released the funds within fifteen days, Elance sends numerous reminders.

I once waited ten days for a client to release *escrow*. All my other clients—and there are many—have released funds within 48 hours. This is typical if you carefully vet clients as we talked about.

Projects with Milestones

The procedure for projects with *milestones* is almost identical to that of projects without *milestones*.

The main difference is you upload your *milestone* documents and mark the *milestone* as *complete*. The *Add to Billing* box will show a checkmark when you mark the milestone complete. Add any comments required to the comment box and click *submit*.

You request *escrow* funding for the next milestone, if it has not already been funded. Once funding is received, you work towards your next *milestone*. Once completed, upload your documents, mark the *milestone complete,* add comments, and *submit.* You repeat this process until you reach the deliverable date. Upload the final documents, mark the project *complete*, say "thank you", and *submit.*

You receive an email notification from Elance when *escrow* is funded for each *milestone*. You receive a further notification when the client has released *escrow* funds. You can withdraw your money under the subtab *Withdraw Funds* located under the main tab *Manage* at the top of your home screen.

Dispute Resolution

Dispute Resolution is available on fixed price projects only. A *Dispute* can be filed by either party if funds have not been released from *escrow* or were released within thirty days prior to filing of the *Dispute. Dispute Resolution* is intended as a method for the parties to come to a resolution. Elance does not make a decision for either party.

You fill out a *Dispute Notice* form detailing the nature of the disagreement and the resolution you seek. There is a two business day grace period after filing the *Dispute Notice* for you and the client to come to an agreement.

If this does not happen, Elance contacts you and the client to set up a *dispute* call with an Elance facilitator. This is logistically your last opportunity to come to an agreement. Once again, the facilitator is there to encourage a resolution between you and the client. The facilitator does not make a final and binding decision.

Should the *dispute* remain unresolved after the facilitation call, your only option is *Arbitration*. The reason I say the facilitation call is your last viable step is because *Arbitration* involves costs. Dependent on the arbitration company used and which party requests *Arbitration*, this process can cost hundreds of dollars. This is where you have to weigh the pros and cons and make a judgment on whether it is worth the costs.

I have never been involved in a *dispute*. However, hypothetically if I was, the project would have to be worth a substantial sum to make it worth expending the extra arbitration costs. There are no guarantees with *arbitration*. You might win, partially win, or lose. It is a risk venture that should be considered carefully before proceeding.

Terms of Service
I highly recommend you peruse Elance's Terms of Service and Code of Conduct to ensure you are not in contravention of any policies.

Future Elance Initiatives
Elance bought out oDesk in 2014. At the time, Elance

stated Elance and oDesk would continue as two separate entities. News received February 25, 2015 reveals that, in fact, Elance has plans to the contrary. Elance is developing a bridge between the two platforms that will be available "within a year or two."

Quick Summary

- Search for *fixed price* projects
- Submit *proposals* to vetted clients
- Finalize *terms and conditions* (make sure the client is paying the Elance fees)
- Request *escrow* funding
- Work on projects when *escrow* is funded
- Send *status reports* every Sunday by 12 AM Eastern Time
- Deliver documents on appointed *milestones* and mark *milestones* complete on *status reports*
- Request funding for next *milestone*
- Deliver by final deliverable date and mark project complete
- Withdraw funds when *escrow* is released

This is a wrap for the Elance overview. It does not encompass every Elance feature, as there are numerous options and tools that are not applicable to writing for *fixed price* projects.

The next chapter can make or break your career.

CHAPTER 19
PRACTICE DUE DILIGENCE

"Change is certain. Progress is not."
~ E.H. Carr, From Napoleon to Stalin, and Other Essays,
1980

From the outset of writing this book, my goal was to prevent freelancers making the same mistakes I did. My primary purpose is to assist you in commencing a successful career in a matter of weeks.

A Cautionary Tale

If you have read sequentially up to this point, you know the book was not written chronologically. This chapter was to be my last chapter written. It was intended to be an overview of Guru, written in much the same vein as the Elance chapter.

I wrote a few paragraphs, and then logged onto Guru to explore the site with you and explain the system. What I discovered shocked me to the core—Guru no longer offers the quantity and quality of freelance writing projects.

I found only 45 freelance writing projects (compared to approximately 1,400 on Elance) posted by about 75 percent unknown clients, who have never used Guru before.

What was I going to do now? A major chapter of my

book was no longer relevant. I pondered this situation for a few days and asked my nonfiction colleagues for advice.

We collaborated and the next chapters are what we decided upon. So far, I have advised you on all the right steps to take, but I have not paid attention to important issues such as due diligence, diversity, and social media.

I intend to rectify these oversights in this and the following two chapters. I believe it strengthens your knowledge base and decision-making processes—all for the better.

What is Due Diligence?

There are many situations in life where we have to practice due diligence—choosing a school for our children, purchasing a vehicle, buying a home, signing insurance and other legal documents or contracts.

The Merriam-Oxford Dictionary defines due diligence as: research and analysis of a company or organization done in preparation for a business transaction.

That same due diligence applies to your career as a freelance writer. You need to keep your finger on the pulse of the freelance writing world. That means staying on top of current news surrounding existing and startup freelance websites.

We need to know who the major players in the game are. It is imperative you realize when a freelance website is in trouble, so you can take proactive steps to protect your sources of income.

Let us take the example of Guru. What happened? Did the competition swallow their market share? Or?

Guru began operations in 1999. For a number of years, it was the largest freelance marketplace. Over its history, it has conducted $100,000 million in transactions.

One review I read opines Guru lost its market share due to the lack of positive reviews of the site, and complaints to the Better Business Bureau have exacerbated the situation.

The comment below was posted in late 2013 in response to another review I read. It is paraphrased as the blog owner did not respond to my request for permission to reprint the comment:

> "Guru has more scams, with few ways of prevention. Escrow accounts have been changed to Safepay. FAQs are not updated. Contact links have been rerouted to an unmonitored "Answers" forum. The freelance side of the operation was updated in December. Bugs are reported daily, but Guru either ignores the reports or states 'it's not high priority'. There are only three staff. No announcements are made regarding updates. Freelancers have no voice in decisions made. Guru is more concerned with competition than rectifying malfunctions."

This freelancer obviously saw the writing on the wall. The fact that escrow protection was dropped is a huge red flag. Never work where escrow is not offered. Otherwise, you could end up owing. A freelancer blogged he was paid via an e-check from the client payable to Guru and the money was released to him by Guru. Almost three weeks later, Guru informed him the e-check was NSF and demanded repayment of more than $700.

I also found posts from previous Guru clients who state Guru dropped them for no apparent reason, without recourse for appeal or conversation.

Another factor is the ".com bust" in March, 2010. Numerous freelance websites bit the dust, with a limited number of survivors. I am not entirely convinced this is the largest factor in Guru's decline. Maltreatment of clients and freelancers, and lack of support for freelancers are arguably the greatest causes.

Guru revamped its entire system during early 2014. It could be Guru is attempting to regain its market share and attract clients and freelancers with the new format. Whether this is successful remains to be seen.

The Guru scenario reinforced my usual tactics regarding freelance sites. Startups are common and I have researched them since 2008. You must undertake due diligence before wasting your time and money on a freelance site that is not viable. After all, you are trying to earn a living freelance writing.

This is part and parcel of owning a business and self-employment. You have to look out for yourself and ensure you recognize warning signs before you fall into what may be dire circumstances through lack of knowledge.

Quick Summary

- Stay on top of current news regarding freelance income sites
- Know who the top players are
- Carefully monitor your writing sources to ensure they remain viable, are proactive in attracting business, supportive of freelance writers, and have an escrow system that prevents clients from nonpayment after you have delivered a project
- Ignore due diligence at your peril

The next topic to be addressed is diversity. Flip the page!

CHAPTER 20
DIVERSIFICATION—COVERING YOUR OPTIONS

"He may well win the race that runs by himself."
~ Benjamin Franklin, Poor Richard's Almanac, 1747

Adding diversity to the mix might garner you clients that become regular customers.

For this reason, I am including brief overviews of additional freelance sites where you might happen upon a worthwhile project. Most of these sites have projects that pay extremely low (as in $3 per hour). Oftentimes, the clients indicate only South East Asia residents need apply.

I received a message recently from a hopeful client on oDesk informing me I was a perfect fit for their needs and offering me a permanent job. Problem was, I know nothing about IT. Nor will I work 40 hours a week for $250 USD monthly.

However, one of my mentoring students was able to quit her day job based on contracts received through oDesk. This may be attributable, in part, to her professional background, which she has been able to capitalize on. The same may be true for you.

While I believe you need backup options, do not spend a copious amount of time digging through numerous websites in the hopes of finding a pearl amongst the pebbles.

Skim these freelance sites, rather than clicking on every project. There is enough information in the preview to indicate the budget, project parameters, the percentage of projects the client awards, how much the client has spent, and freelancers' feedback to make a decision on whether to further investigate. The idea is to spend more time working, less time submitting proposals on undesirable projects.

Upwork (formerly oDesk)

oDesk is owned by Elance, but for the time being the websites operate as separate entities. Elance is working to "bridge" oDesk and Elance. There will be several forthcoming changes in the near future that will eventually sync both platforms. The name Upwork was instituted May 5, 2015. As changed are implemented, you can reference Chapter 18 Elance Overview.

At the time of publication, there are no membership fees; a ten percent fee is billed to the client. This means you never pay a fee to oDesk. It is the client's responsibility.

You need a work-only email address and a Skype account.

There is a job application quota restriction on oDesk. This is determined by whether you have taken the basic *oDesk Readiness Test*. You only receive a quota of two job applications without this test. You can increase your quota by taking tests. Feedback also is a factor in the number of job applications you are permitted. The higher the feedback, the more job applications you are allowed.

There are free skills tests available to illustrate your competency.

The formal route for obtaining work on oDesk is:

- Apply for a project with a cover letter, your rate, and attachments

- The client contacts freelancers for interviews
- A paid test may be requested.

You can offer to work for the client for an hour at your specified rate of pay as a "test project".

If the client requests an interview, these are conducted via:

- oDesk Message Center
- Skype
- Phone

Personally, I have great reservations about disclosing my personal phone number for security reasons. I recommend *oDesk Message Center* and Skype only.

Interviews are a two-way street. Think of the interview as a method of determining whether you want to work with the client. Ask questions; state your expectations. Of course, you want to sell your services, but not at the expense of working with a client who is difficult, underpays, or has unrealistic expectations. A tip: When you approach an interview from this perspective, it alleviates your nerves.

Not all clients interview freelancers; some outright award projects. You can monitor the award process by checking the job post periodically to discover if freelancers are being interviewed and whether the job has been awarded.

Only hourly projects are covered by the *oDesk Guarantee*. *Fixed price* project payments are at the client's discretion, which I consider too high risk. Also, there are few *fixed price* projects posted.

Once you are awarded a project, create a *contract* detailing your agreement with the client, including your pay rate. Projects without *contracts* are not covered by the oDesk Guarantee.

To work hourly projects on oDesk, you need to download the *Team App* to enter your hours. The app takes screenshots every ten minutes. You are permitted to delete screenshots you do not want the client to view. Clients are permitted to set a maximum number of hours per week.

The workweek ends on Saturdays. You and the client finalize your *time logs* and you receive payment ten days later.

I am not a fan of hourly projects with "Big Brother screenshots", however, oDesk is a marketplace for more than projects. If you are interested in working full- or part-time or on a temporary contract, there are many job offers on tap.

Freelanced.com

You can apply to any projects without restrictions for a reasonable annual fee. This is not a freelance website that provides escrow or invoice services.

You set up your profile and upload documents to your profile. I recommend you include your resume in the portfolio as the message board does not have the capability to attach documents.

Freelanced.com advertises itself as a Freelance Social Network. You can accumulate kudos and friends. You are permitted to list up to twelve skills.

If the client hires you, all financial details are handled between you and the client. I highly recommend you invoice through PayPal, with a fifty percent deposit and the remaining 50 percent upon delivery of the project. Include PayPal service fees in your invoice.

There are a limited number of projects available but, every so often, an attractive opportunity is posted. You can also set up email alerts for projects that fit within your skillset.

WriteJobs

This site does not post numerous positions. There is an average of three to five per day. They may also be duplicate postings found on other sites.

You must apply and meet qualifications to be hired.

FlexJobs

FlexJobs is a marketplace for freelance professionals. You pay FlexJobs a monthly fee to offer you global leads for freelance positions. FlexJobs claims to weed out the scam artists and only promote quality, verified leads.

You can pay monthly, for a three month period, or yearly. FlexJobs is suited for individuals who are looking for permanent or temporary positions with clients, rather than on short-term projects.

A drawback is many positions require a degree or a specified number of years' experience in a particular field. FlexJobs may not be suitable as this guidebook is intended for aspiring freelance writers without the need for higher education. However, should you happen to have a degree and want to parlay it into writing, FlexJobs might be of benefit.

Magazine Pitches

While this book is focused on freelance writing websites where you receive guaranteed payment upon completion of a project, there are opportunities through other sources. These involve sending pitches for article ideas and/or articles to magazines.

There is no guarantee your work will be accepted, and it can take weeks or months (if ever) to hear back whether your pitch or article is accepted. If your pitch or article is accepted, often payment is not received until it is published. This can be another several months down the line.

While this is not a secure, steady, flow of income, you might be interested in sending pitches while you are working on projects that guarantee you income at the end of the project.

Sample query letters for freelance writers for various interests or fields can be found at http://www.freelancewriting.com/sample-query-letters-for-writers.php

Writing Career

Writing Career (which is operated by FreelanceWriting.com) has a "Call for Submissions" section in the upper right corner. Click on the appropriate Call for Submissions to browse available prospects.

Check the top of the submission page to see when it was last updated. Also, each submission gives a deadline, along with an indication of the pay rate. The rates can be quite attractive, however; you have to win the pitch and be published. Competition can be fierce for higher paying clients.

There are countless other freelance writing schemes in cyberland. I have not included them all, because they are one or several of the following:

- low-paying
- restrict the number of proposals you can submit
- restrict you to a certain pay level until you have submitted "x" number of articles or received "y" number of reviews
- pay on graduated scale
- revenue sharing
- bogus

Quick Summary

- Diversity offers the potential of additional clients
- Backup options are necessities
- Do not spend inordinate time searching backup options

Startups are common. The online writing world is in a constant state of flux. Make sure you practice due diligence. Do not pay membership fees for startups. If it does not feel right; follow your instinct.

CHAPTER 21
SOCIAL MEDIA—DO I HAVE TO?

"Laissez faire."
~ Marquis d'Aregenson, Memoires, 1736

Social media is unavoidable, but this does not mean you need to spend a lot of time interacting on a multitude of platforms. Rather, you need to develop an "in and out" attitude, gleaning useful information and logging out. Social media can be a huge time suck that takes away from productive writing hours.

I have not observed engaging in social media is particularly productive in terms of obtaining gigs, but you can learn valuable tips and information from various groups.

Facebook

There are a few groups you can join on Facebook and chat with other freelance writers. Their experiences can be of benefit to you; you may discover what is working or not working from other freelancers.

These include:

- Facebook4Freelancers.com : Freelance Writing Jobs : Freelancing Group
- Write Jobs
- Freelance Writers

- Writers of Non-Fiction (although the focus in on writing nonfiction books, there are a number of freelance writers who are members of this group)

LinkedIn

LinkedIn is—in my opinion—the best platform for freelance writers to participate in groups to discuss freelance writing issues, opportunities and scams, setting rates, improving writing skills, and many other topics.

Suggested groups are:
- Newbie Freelance Writers
- The Freelance Writers Team
- Freelance Writers

You set up your profile on LinkedIn by filling in the blanks. It automatically populates a complete profile and resume by prompting you to complete information.

One warning: scams abound on LinkedIn in groups by unscrupulous members attempting to bring new freelance writers onboard. Double, triple, quadruple check and research job postings. Some are bogus; some pay $1 per 500 words. Ask the poster insightful questions about their operation. Often, they do not reply because it is a scam, and they have no evidence to back up answers to your questions.

I contacted one outfit via their online chat board and explained I was writing this book and would like to know more about their operation. The response was enthusiastic. I asked if I might call a representative. I was told the CEO was too busy, but to send her an email outlining my questions. I did so, and never heard from her.

I was fortunate to connect with a writer on LinkedIn who worked with this service. She told me it was her worst agency experience ever and she was paid $0.0075 per word. That is ¾ of a cent per word. Hardly a living wage.

Recently, I was contacted by a bona fide company and added to their team. I now work with the company on a contract basis.

You can also search for jobs on LinkedIn. I periodically receive emails from LinkedIn with employment opportunity suggestions.

It is not worthwhile spending money on an upgraded membership. Although LinkedIn constantly touts the benefits, I have been assured by a LinkedIn expert the free membership is more than sufficient. Aside from that advice, paid membership is expensive.

Quick Summary

- Social media is a necessity
- You should not spend a lot of time on social media
- Join relevant groups
- Develop an "in and out" attitude
- Only read what may be of value
- Do chat briefly
- Facebook and LinkedIn are the best social media platforms for freelance writers
- LinkedIn offers job searches
- Do not pay for upgraded LinkedIn
- Scams abound on LinkedIn—do your due diligence

The Next Chapter...

CHAPTER 22
THE NEXT CHAPTER

"I have seen the future and it works."
~ Lincoln Steffens, letter to Marie Howe, April 3, 1919

This really is the next chapter in your life. You are set to commence a new career as a professional freelance writer. I place heavy emphasis on "professional". You are a professional, much the same as any occupation. Keep this designation in mind at all times, and it will serve you well.

Resist those clients who attempt to treat you as less than a professional. A few believe they are the king headpin and treat you as a lowly subordinate. You are the ultimate boss and director of your professional career. If you come across job descriptions where the client has this type of attitude, carry on. They are not worth it and will cause you nothing but headaches. You do not need these clients to take away your joy and pride in your abilities.

Have confidence you have the knowledge and tools necessary for success. Because you do. Believe in yourself wholeheartedly. Your confidence and professional approach will impress clients. Clients love a take-charge professional who gives them exactly what they need.

Where you go from here and what you accomplish is up to you. Dedicate yourself, and you will be a success. Strive to learn at all times. But, above all, enjoy your work.

Freelance Writing Express is a thorough guide to freelance writing success. Freelance websites periodically upgrade their systems and practices. When major updates are rolled out, I will revise this edition to encompass the new standards. You will automatically receive the revised edition through Amazon's Whispersync.

I am at the finish line of this journey, and you are in the starting chute of your journey. An exciting moment!

Thank you for purchasing this book. It was written with the intent of assisting aspiring freelance writers achieve success in optimal time. I know this will happen for you.

Amazon Reviews

I would appreciate a few seconds of your time to leave a review on Amazon. Reviews are the bread and butter of authors, much the same as client reviews are for freelance writers. I began as a freelance writer, which led me to write this book. Who knows? Maybe someday you will discover the urge to write a book based on your expertise.

I welcome your questions, thoughts, and comments. My email address is darleneelizabethwilliams @outlook.com. I respond to all emails.

My best wishes for your success,

Darlene Elizabeth Williams
Freelance Writer & Mentor
Copy Editor & Proofreader
Fiction & Nonfiction Author

Social Media Links:

Website:
http://darleneelizabethwilliamsauthor.com/

Facebook:

https://www.facebook.com/DarleneEWilliams

Facebook (*Freelance Writing Express*):

https://www.facebook.com/pages/Freelance-Writing-Express-How-to-Earn-Money-Within-Two-Weeks/592696114079476:

https://www.facebook.com/DarleneEWilliams

Twitter:

https://www.facebook.com/DarleneEWilliams

LinkedIn:

https://www.linkedin.com/pub/darlene-elizabeth-williams/5a/888/861